"WRITTEN IN GOOD SPIRIT ...

Emphasizes that each mourner or afflicted individual has special needs ... Of interest to many diverse readers."

Boston Herald

"[Donnelley] addresses everything from the grief felt with the death of an aged parent and the terminal illness of a child to the pain of divorce and the loss of a job. Special attention is also given to the needs of children in mourning."

Good News

"Invaluable ... Engrossing ... Donnelley writes with sensitivity and compassion."

Union City Messenger (Tennessee)

"In compassionate and loving terms, Donnelley has brought death into the light, giving us the resources to never again be in the position of not knowing what to say or do."

Gainesville Sun (Florida)

Also by Nina Herrmann Donnelley
Published by Ballantine Books:

GO OUT IN JOY!

I NEVER KNOW WHAT TO SAY

Nina Herrmann Donnelley

BALLANTINE BOOKS • NEW YORK

Library of Congress Catalog Card Number: 86-47847

ISBN 0-345-36519-4

Manufactured in the United States of America

First Hardcover Edition: April 1987
First Mass Market Edition: September 1990

This book is dedicated

To—

Aleka, Audrey, C.J., Aunt Dot and Uncle Gay, Dr. Davies, Ellie, Hector, Henry, Fr. Jim, J.B. IV, John, Jorie, Leslie, Lynda, Nancy, Nancye, Nicole, Niel, Ray, Ruth Ann, and many others over the years . . . who have taught me about friendship by being my friends.

To—

Daddy, Marty, and Aunt Ann . . . who urged (badgered?) me for years to ''write another book.''

And especially to—

Jim . . . who not only ''urged'' but also provided the space and the place.

—Love and thanks to you all!

CONTENTS

ACKNOWLEDGMENTS

As always, my love and thanks to my mother and father for planting the seeds of my faith . . .

And my gratitude to Dr. Elam Davies—preacher, lecturer, and Pastor Emeritus of the Fourth Presbyterian Church of Chicago—who nurtured that faith.

Many thanks, too, to Dr. Martin Marty of the Divinity School of the University of Chicago, who read the first draft of this book and offered many helpful suggestions . . .

To Beth Rashbaum of Ballantine Books who did a superb job of editing the manuscript . . . .

And to Mary Gerard who typed the final draft(s!) and Beverly Riedy who transcribed it "in the rough."

1

A Death

CHRIS WAS FIFTY. I was thirty-one. He was a staunch Roman Catholic. I was studying to be a Presbyterian minister.

We had been dating with steadily increasing interest despite our age and denominational differences for about a year and a half. I don't know if it was "true love"; but I do know that Chris and I were happy and content in each other's company.

On a Wednesday evening in October, Chris and I had gone to a political dinner. The speaker was boring beyond tears. So, while fixing my eyes on the podium, I planned a dream trip to Europe, as is my custom during all boring speeches and Wagner operas. I also slipped off my right shoe and, under cover of the nearly floor-length tablecloth, surreptitiously inserted my stockinged toes beneath Chris's trouser cuff and rubbed them up and down his leg, as was my custom whenever dining with Chris.

Chris kept a straight face, never flinching, though I knew he was terribly ticklish, and whispered with the threat of annihilation in his voice, "Stop that!" Naturally, I didn't.

Afterwards, to recover from the speech, we stopped at a favorite place for a drink, where we talked and just enjoyed being with each other.

Chris had bony knees—really bony. Strange what in one person attracts another! I always enjoyed pounding on his bony knees with my fist.

As we were driving home that Wednesday, stopped for a red light, I was pounding Chris's right knee and laughing. Chris was delivering his usual response—how he couldn't understand the humor I derived from his knees.

We parked in front of my apartment building. It was late. "I'm not even going to kiss you good night," he announced teasingly. "I'm coming down with a cold, and not being thoughtless like those others you date. . . ." I laughed and we walked to the door and shook hands good night. After all, we would see each other the next day, and would be going out again on Friday.

Chris and I always went out on Friday nights, like clockwork; an understanding of sorts. We worked in the same office, Chris as an executive and I as a part-time administrative assistant en route through divinity school and chaplaincy training. We worked hard at keeping our relationship platonic at work, and no one knew we dated as often or liked each other as much as we did.

Our offices were across from each other. And on Friday afternoons, after closing, I would go to Chris's office, mostly bothering him as he finished up, and then we would go out for a long, relaxing dinner. I loved Fridays.

But the Friday following that Wednesday in October Chris didn't come to work. His secretary told me he had left word for me that he had to go out of town. That really wasn't like Chris. But he had mentioned on Wednesday that he would be going away soon on business. So I assumed he just had to go early.

With nothing else to do that night, I decided to go grocery shopping so I could sleep later the next morning. That accomplished, I watched television a bit and read. I was just considering turning off the light when the telephone rang, about 11:10 P.M. It was my boss's secretary. She was one of the few people in the office who knew that Chris and I dated at all.

"Are you sitting down?" Her voice sounded odd.

"Yes?"

"Oh, I wish I could be there . . . something terrible has happened. . . ."

My boss was in Europe on vacation and since it was his secretary calling, I immediately pictured him dead in a plane crash.

"Are you strong?" she asked.

"Yes—what *is* it? Tell me!"

"Chris is dead."

It was the last thing I expected. My mind wasn't even in the neighborhood.

The lady who telephoned understandably didn't enjoy being a messenger of death. After adding some details and being assured that I was "all right," she hung up quickly.

I did not move, not a muscle, for I'm not sure how long; maybe fifteen minutes, maybe longer.

Then I needed to talk to someone, needed to tell someone, needed to say the words.

Of several friends who came to mind, one was the mother of a little girl who had died about a year and a half earlier, while I was chaplain at a children's hospital. We had become close friends during her child's illness and death, and had remained close friends since. Jane Miles and her husband had met Chris, and we had been to their home. Jane would understand.

Jane listened to me for an hour—an hour *beginning* at about 11:30 that night. No complaints or hesitations despite the time and length of the call. *She just listened*, and she and her husband offered to do anything they could, and said they would call the next morning.

But after all that, after an hour of talking to a friend who listened and understood, I found I had to say it yet again. I had to hear the words come out of my mouth again. For when nothing was said, it wasn't real.

I repeated the story to Jennifer Bradford, another friend who is a nurse on a pediatric neurosurgery unit. She, too, listened for nearly another hour and offered to come or do anything she could. And she said she would call tomorrow . . . which was today.

Finally I turned out the light that night. But now it wouldn't have mattered. I just lay there, awake, staring at the ceiling.

According to the woman who had called me, Chris hadn't gone out of town at all. He had had bad chest pains Friday morning and had gone to the hospital. It was diagnosed as a mild heart attack. He was put into the Coronary Intensive Care Unit. He hadn't wanted me to know or worry. As I said, he was about twenty years older than I. He called me "kid."

At 8:30 that Friday evening, suddenly, in the middle of the Coronary Intensive Care Unit, Chris had a massive heart attack. He died less than one hour later. There was nothing they could do, even in the middle of the C.I.C.U.

A few weeks earlier that October, Chris and I had been having our perpetual "devout Catholic versus liberal Presbyterian" argument about works and grace and the "earnability" of salvation. Purgatory had crept into the conversation.

"You know what I'm worried about?" Chris had said. "I'm worried that by the time I die nobody will be around to pray me out of purgatory."

I laughed. "Well, Christopher, I'll pray you through!" I said, pounding his bony knee.

"Do you mean that? Will you?" He was serious.

"Yes," I said, not laughing any more. "If you think a Presbyterian can do any good—especially one who doesn't believe in purgatory at all."

"I'll take all the help I can get." He definitely was serious. It gave me the shivers.

But that Friday night as I lay awake in bed, I literally prayed for Chris to get through purgatory. I prefaced each prayer with "God, I don't believe in this, but . . . ." But I prayed for Chris's Catholic soul, nonetheless.

I'm not sure, though, whether it was purgatory I didn't believe in that night, or the *fact* that I was now trying to pray a dead Chris through it.

If I was going to replace denial with acceptance of fact, something still had to happen to really prove to me that Chris was dead. So Saturday morning I went out and bought a newspaper. If I saw it in print it would be fact and then I would accept it, of course.

I did—see it in print, that is. But it was just words on paper. And the photograph was terrible. I read the obituary and threw the paper aside. I had my printed confirmation. But I didn't want to see it. Or believe it.

Other than going out to buy the paper, I didn't move that Saturday. I called my parents and my minister and recited the facts of Chris's death. And friends called me—Jane and Jennifer and others—and I was glad, though I didn't remember what they said and didn't want them to come to be with me.

Mostly I just sat in bed. I was indulging myself in mourning, I decided, getting it over with all in one day. A benefit of the death and dying training I had received on the way to becoming a hospital chaplain.

But as I sat there in bed that Saturday, one thing I wasn't prepared for was my vague sense of anger. I didn't *feel* any anger. But thoughts edged with anger were going through my head—*anger at Chris for dying*. This simply was not the right time for him to do such a thing. I don't know if Chris and I would have married or not, but now he had died, so we wouldn't have a chance to find out.

But marriage thoughts weren't uppermost in my mind that morning. What I could not stop thinking about were all the everyday kinds of expectations which would now be chopped off because Chris had died: regular Friday dinners and other dates; autumn day trips into brilliantly colored woods; bicycle rides and pumpkin carving and pumpkin pies; Thanksgiving and Christmas; tree chopping and gift shopping and snowball fights; warm fires and mistletoe and s'mores! How Chris hated s'mores!

If Chris really was dead; if Chris had allowed himself to die despite all the physical fitness he was into; if Chris really was dead, how could we still do all these things? I had been cheated. *Chris* had cheated me. His timing was wrong. It wasn't fair—not fair of him to die, not now.

Still, I didn't *feel* anger. Nor did I *feel* sympathy for his brother and sister and mother. Nor did I *feel* overwhelming sadness for Chris, the man who had died.

I didn't feel any of these things. I merely thought these things. For still, after everything—after being told it, telling it to others, and reading about it in print—still Chris being dead just didn't feel real. It was a fact only "out there" somewhere. Not inside of me.

Nonetheless, I stayed home Saturday and mourned. That was what I was supposed to do, after all, I knew from my death and dying training.

There was something else that Saturday and Saturday night that went through my mind: a kaleidoscope of imagined pictures, imagined scenes, and questions. I couldn't stop picturing, wondering—what did the Cardiac Intensive Care Unit at Wickham Memorial Hospital, where Chris died, look like? What floor was it on? Where was his bed? Was it in one large room, like Children's Hospital where I studied? Did Chris have tubes and monitors? Were there lots of doctors and nurses working on him? Did the priest give him last rites?

And what about Chris? What did he look like? Was he awake?

Was he in pain? Was he alone? What if he died alone? Did he know he was dying? What did he say, and to whom? Was he afraid? Those imagined images and scenes and all those questions played frenzied and futile leapfrog through my mind throughout the long hours of that Saturday.

Sunday morning I told myself I had slept the night before, and I was fine now. I had prayed Chris on his way through purgatory; I believed he was in heaven; and I had completely accepted his death. I had successfully mourned in one day and two nights.

I still had not wept.

I think I went to the Art Institute Sunday and then took some prints to a shop to be framed. But really I don't remember, other than that I was *sure* the worst was over.

On Monday I went to the office—the office where Chris had always waved to me, and stuck his head in my door, and called "Hi, kid," and told me about his successes—and his fears. The office where the two of us had spent bits of many days talking and joking and sharing.

I could overhear the conversations as people came to talk with Chris's secretary. It built, the pressure in my head, until I couldn't go on. I told my boss's secretary I was leaving early. She seemed to understand. But no one else did. Their eyes said, "Hey, what's your problem? Why do you think you're so special? We'll all miss him around here."

It never ceases to amaze me how ready we are to judge one another, to decide what would be appropriate for another to feel.

I didn't want to go to Chris's wake, and didn't want to view the body. If all those other people were right, and he really was dead, I would much rather remember his grin as we shook hands good night on Wednesday, I reasoned. That's the picture of him I wanted to remember. But even though everybody kept telling me he was dead, I still had to prove it to myself. And I think I knew deep down that the only way to believe it was to see him dead.

I took a bus to Jennifer's home to borrow her car. She had offered it several times in our talks since Chris had died. But I never processed that I would need it until I actually needed it. I remember the bus ride to her apartment. Everyone on the bus was acting so normal; laughing or complaining about dumb things. Didn't they know Chris had died? I wanted to scream at them to shut up, to stop . . . to simply stop. But I didn't.

It didn't help that the large funeral home turned out to be almost directly across the street from a restaurant where Chris and I had gone on one of our happiest dates. I parked the car and went inside and asked for directions. My senses walked backward as my legs walked forward.

I got to the back viewing room door and stopped. I could hear some people inside talking quietly, leaving. I peeked around the corner and jumped back, all in one motion—the second half preservation instinct, like putting your finger on a hot stove. I grabbed the door frame and held on. No, oh no. No.

I can remember at least two of our dates that began with Chris "stopping off for a minute" to attend a friend's wake. It was a matter of respect in his eyes. That's why I didn't leave. I had seen, I had the proof. The people were right. Chris was dead. I could have left. But the respect. . . .

Chris had joked about his own wake, about being "laid out, American flag and all." And now he was. The joke was real. I looked around the corner again. This time in two motions. But I still couldn't go in.

Finally, holding my stomach, I walked in. The other people had gone. There was a kneeling bench by the side of the coffin. I was glad. I couldn't have stood. My body had gone numb.

He looked all right, I supposed; but it surely wasn't the face with the grin. And his blue eyes—his best feature—were closed, shut off. Only his hair, his gray hair, looked real.

I closed my eyes and said a few purgatory prayers, and a few other things. Then I opened my eyes and they fell on Chris's hands. His fingers were clenched around a huge black rosary. They had the look of desperation, not of peace.

I wanted to touch his hair, but I settled for his arm. The jacket sleeve crinkled as though it had plastic wrap under it. Suddenly I had visions that only his head was in the casket, stuffed inside the shirt of an effigy. I shuddered and got up quickly.

Two of Chris's nieces were at the door, but I couldn't speak beyond a word or two. My body had ceased existing at the stump of my throat. But I only realized this when I went to sign the guest book and I couldn't write.

I found Jennifer's car, sat in it and breathed. Just breathed.

Then, because it was scheduled, I drove to the University of

Chicago for a meeting. But it took me on and off the whole way there to remember and retain *why* I had to be there.

The minister/professor with whom I had a meeting accepted my label "friend"—"my friend died"—in the customary sense and passed over my grief perfunctorily, with traditional words of sympathy and no further questions. Granted, I wasn't being fair to him, trying to keep a normal appointment in a far-from-normal condition. But I couldn't comprehend that then.

I remember nothing else of that day.

Jane and Jennifer and other friends offered to go to Chris's funeral with me on Tuesday. But being sure I not only had gotten over the worst of Chris's death but also had accepted it, I said no, I'd be "all right." It was a mistake: I hadn't, I hadn't, and I wasn't.

During the funeral mass I didn't make a sound. But about halfway into the service suddenly a steady stream of tears started that I could not stop, no matter how hard I tried—and I tried very hard. Soon my head was so stuffed I couldn't breathe.

The old Catholic church had a lot of steps down from the main entrance to the curb. Chris had joked many times about pitying those who would have to carry his casket down the steep incline. After the services I stayed inside the church until I was sure it was over, until I was sure Chris's casket was at the bottom of those steps. But I may as well have watched. I couldn't get the picture of him laughing about it out of my mind. I could see the pallbearers without even looking.

It was a long, long drive from the church in the city to the Roman Catholic cemetery in the suburbs. I was all right driving along alone . . . all right until I remembered Chris's bony knee, and that I never would be able to pound on it again.

That did it. I guess something had to. My "jungle of emotions" burst, and I sobbed, alone, isolated, clutching the steering wheel, driving unseeing, for a long, long time. Oh, how I suddenly needed someone to be there, someone to hold on to.

The graveside service wasn't. It was held in a chapel and was very brief. I guess it's supposed to be less painful that way. But it wasn't so for me. I felt a sense of something unfinished. I didn't even know where Chris's grave was.

After the service the priest announced that everyone was invited by the family to a nearby restaurant for lunch. But I didn't go. I went, instead, to the cemetery office to find where Chris was to be buried. They gave me a map of the cemetery and circled a rectangle where his plot was.

I drove up to it. No one else was there. The casket was still in the chapel, I guess. The hole had been dug and was covered by an old board. I could look down into the dark hollow through a chipped corner of the board.

I had to *do* something, something to make Chris feel "welcome," not alone, not forgotten when he got there. I reached into my purse and tore off a corner from the back inside page of my address book. I pressed the small white paper to my lips. The lipstick transferred. A kiss. I dropped it into the black, empty hole, and got into Jennifer's car and drove away.

Jane Miles—the first friend I talked to the night Chris died— had made me promise to come to her home, near the cemetery, after the burial. I don't remember the drive. I do remember she had a large drink waiting for me when I got there, the effects of which I didn't feel. And she listened. She once again listened to me for several hours.

But as I talked I became increasingly uneasy. I felt I had to go back to the cemetery. I felt I had to be sure Chris was "safe," was buried at last . . . had found the kiss. I didn't tell Jane that, about the kiss, only that I wanted to stop by the cemetery again before it closed. She understood. She had buried her nine-year-old daughter eighteen months earlier.

A young man was closing the cemetery gates as I arrived. I'm sure I looked desperate, perhaps crazed. "I have to go in, please. He just got here today. I have to see the grave . . . I'll just be a minute, I promise."

I love that young man in a corner of my heart somewhere. He could have said no. But he didn't. He opened the gate.

I drove quickly to the grave and ran up the knoll. Fresh dirt covered the hole. The familiar rectangle. Chris was inside. Chris was underneath. With the kiss. Safe. Not alone.

The young man drove slowly by in a gray truck. I got in the car and followed him to a back exit.

Thank you, young man.

I drove back to the city. But there was still something I had to do before I could go home. Something of Chris's I had to get.

I went to the office. A few people were still there, but no one saw me. I went into Chris's office. It looked empty, dusty, though nothing had been removed, including what I had come for. It was there, still up on his bookshelf: a child's toy, a white stuffed goat wearing a red, white, and green button that read "Kid Power!" I had given Chris the goat and the button because he always called me "kid." "Hi, kid."

I nestled the soft little toy under my arm and left. No one noticed. I drove home.

At home in my mail that Tuesday evening I found a sympathy card from Jennifer. That card meant as much to me as anything else that day. It was something tangible to say, "Yes, you are a mourner. Yes, a friend can mourn a friend. Yes, it's okay to mourn."

The next day, Wednesday, I took a "vacation" day. I drove in Jennifer's car back to the suburban cemetery. With me I took a small seat cushion, a book, and a magazine.

When I arrived there was sod over the plot, but no marker yet and no flowers. Nothing, really, to say that *Chris* was there. Only a faint rectangular outline where the resident grass and the replaced grass hadn't grown together again. Something should say that Chris was there, that the plot was "occupied."

I got back into the car, determined to find plastic flowers that would last until the marker came.

I *hate* plastic flowers. But that morning I wanted them more than any other thing on earth.

I didn't know where to begin. I saw no plastic flower stores near the cemetery. I drove and drove. I stopped at a florist and could find nothing suitable. I drove some more, no longer having any idea where I was going. Finally, miles away, I came upon another cemetery, and across the street was a plastic flower store.

They were awful. But I was determined. Chris was very patriotic. Finally I found a bouquet of red, white, and blue plastic carnations, affixed to a stake, ready to be stuck into the ground. There must be other people like me out there.

I bought them and drove back to Chris's grave. And there, in the suburban Roman Catholic cemetery, atop the freshly sodded plot, right about where its owner's bony knee would be, I placed the bunch of red, white, and blue plastic flowers. They looked rather pretty after all! And they made his grave official.

Then I got my seat cushion, my magazine, and my book and sat with Chris for a while. To make him feel comfortable. To make him feel not alone in a strange place. To make him feel still loved, not forgotten. I sat with him because the rest of the world out there was insisting on going on and somebody had to stay with Chris; somebody had to stop.

I got my seat cushion, my magazine, and my book, and I sat with Chris for a while: four and one half hours.

Death is crazy. . . .

2

Overview

THIS IS A book about mourning. Its purpose is to help the reader better understand the process of mourning. It is not a panacea posing all situations of mourning and offering all answers to all questions. It is a simply worded guide for those who would like to help a friend or relative through the process of mourning death, or dying, or other types of extreme loss, but who often feel they don't know what to say or will say or do the "wrong" thing.

Ideally, it is a book not to be read for the first time by people in the throes of mourning or dying, or trying to help someone who is. Rather, it is a book better read in a time of equilibrium, then used as a resource in time of crisis.

The story of Chris's death and my reaction to it is used not as an example of the ultimate degree or depth of mourning, which it is not; but rather as a case study to help the reader see the mourning process in a definable pattern.

The things that happened in the story are true as I remember them. The fact that I remember them so well is likely based on the nature and length of my relationship with Chris: long enough and deep enough to have offered me a valid reason to mourn his death, but not so long or deep to have made me forever unable to step back and view the process of my mourning.

Generally speaking, the person mourning the death of a child, spouse, or parent will have a rougher road to follow and will not recall the patterns of his mourning so clearly.

All this said, however, I would warn that there is a danger in calibrating the intensity of a person's mourning according to your perception of the length, type, and depth of his relationship with the deceased. For *only* the mourner knows the true value of his relationship and the true degree of loss he is suffering.

If we have typecast the mourner's grief, and if he perceives this, he may try to mourn equal to our expectations, thereby either shortening or extending the time he truly needs to mourn. This can cause harm, especially in cases in which mourning is abbreviated.

A word about mourning in friendship relationships also must be said here. Chris was my friend. I was not related to him through blood or marriage. Nor had we been friends for fifty, or even twenty years.

But a love was operative in the relationship. And in *any* death or loss relationship involving love, some form of mourning will occur.

Many friends truly love each other: man and man, woman and woman, woman and man. The love of friendship can be very deep and immeasurably valuable.

But despite the validity of the love of friend for friend, in most instances there is no sanctioned way of expressing either professional or personal sympathy for the loss of a friend, no greeting cards expressing condolences for such a loss, no discussion of the friend as mourner in most death and dying literature.

In her classic work *On Death and Dying*, Dr. Elisabeth Kubler-Ross devotes a whole chapter to "The Patient's Family" and a section of that chapter to "The Family After Death Has Occurred." In one partial sentence concerning a grieving wife, Dr. Kubler-Ross writes, "The expected assistance from relatives and friends. . . ."

In those few words, Dr. Ross reinforces society's—and the professional's—acceptance chain of mourning: husband dies, wife is to "expect" assistance from relatives and friends.

I do not debate the logic of this, and in most cases it is as it should be. But suppose the wife despised the husband and suppose the husband had a best friend, a buddy with whom he had grown up, attended college, and shared a business? No matter; the friend, in literature and custom, would be expected to "comfort" the wife.

Once I sat on a bus in front of two women discussing the death of a close friend of one of them. The older woman had taken three days off from work to be with the friend who was dying, and to pull herself together afterwards. "Naturally," she said, "I wasn't a relative so I wasn't paid."

North American custom does allow family to mourn for a while, and even react crazily (which I'll speak to later) when a loved one dies. But we rarely, if ever, afford the same privilege to friends. The grieving friend is usually ignored, or expected to perform "comforting acts."

In a later work, *Questions and Answers on Death and Dying*, Dr. Kubler-Ross does acknowledge the grief of friends. When asked, "Do the friends and relatives of a patient go through the five stages the same as he does?" Dr. Kubler-Ross replies, "Yes, anybody who is really involved with a terminally ill patient has to pass through certain adjustment, either prior to death or after death occurs."

". . . anyone who is really involved. . . ." I hope we can remember those words. If someone tells you her friend has just died, give her some room to elaborate, room to tell you if it was more than a casual relationship. If it was a friendship of love, send a sympathy note, and give her some additional chances to talk about her friend if you can. She'll probably be more grateful than you'll ever know.

A major premise of this book is that, from an earthly view, death is irrational, or "crazy." It doesn't make sense for a person to build a life of relationships and loves, and then die, or for a child, new with life, to waste away from cancer. Our logical minds can explain a great deal, but they can't explain the "why" of death. It is illogical. It is irrational. It is crazy.

If death were rational, we would be expected to react to it rationally, with rational words and actions. That would be normal. But if death is irrational, then we can be expected to react to it irrationally, with irrational words and actions. That would be normal.

We do and it is. We do, whether or not we tell anyone, react at times with irrational words and actions to the death of someone we love. And that irrational reaction *is normal*.

I have chosen to call these *normal* irrational reactions to the death of someone we love, "the crazies." I first used the term "crazies"—describing my paper kiss to Chris and my long grave sits—in a speech I gave on death and dying about seven years ago. I did so somewhat hesitantly, fearing I might lose credibility with the audience.

But instead, there was an overwhelming response—not of pity for my abnormal, crazed state, but rather of empathy, followed by numerous examples of similar experiences. Until that night, like me, most of the people in that large audience had never told anyone about their irrational mourning acts for fear of being thought crazy by family or friends.

And it's true: those people, and I, and much of the rest of mankind, do go "crazy" at times during our mourning, *in the sense that we engage in behavior that would appear irrational to someone not in mourning*.

This irrational behavior occurs, however, in reaction to an *irreversible irrational* happening. Death is not rational. It is crazy. Therefore, occasional irrational or "crazy" behavior is a *normal* reaction to death. In other words, it can be normal to behave crazily at times when mourning the death of someone you love.

When he first read the term "crazies," Dr. Martin Marty responded: "I doubt if I could talk you out of it, because you do show that a kind of 'madness' is operative. So it works."

And so, though I readily admit it's not a scholarly term, I use the word "crazies" to describe certain irrational but normal reactions in mourning which will be discussed in more detail later in this book.

Listing stages of behavior patterns in various traumatic life situations has become "in." There are stages of growing up, getting old, and dying, to name a few. Viewing our lives in terms of these stages can help us to see that what may seem frightening or extreme about our responses is actually quite normal. (Dr. Kubler-Ross's books on death and dying, for example, have been immeasurably valuable in this respect.)

A danger in listing behavior in stages, however, is that it can lead some lay people—and some professionals—to categorize others too quickly and too intractably. It can also lead people to assume that everyone goes through each stage of behavior in the exact order presented. This is not always true.

Most professionals, therefore, caution against using any behavioral staging scheme as an absolute. I offer the same advice for the three areas of mourning response I shall discuss in Chapter Three. For each time we are too quick to categorize or label someone we are in danger of ceasing to hear him. And if we don't hear, we cannot help.

For the most part, this book will discuss mourning after death has occurred. When a death comes after a prolonged, terminal illness, some mourning will likely have occurred prior to death, though the amount and degree of that prior mourning will depend on many variables.

It is safe to say, however, that no matter how long the dying or how much the prior grief work, a person will need to go through a period of active mourning following the death of someone he loves. But if that person has done some mourning prior to the death, his "crazies" may not be as pronounced nor his mourning process quite as long.

Because in some respects, the mourning processes are similar, I also discuss briefly in Chapter Seven how to comfort those who have suffered losses besides those occasioned by death. Disability, divorce (or other broken love relationships), even the loss of a job—all are mourned sometimes with surprising intensity. I cannot offer an in-depth study of these losses, just a few guidelines on how to be a friend and "what to say." But it is important to remember that *all* losses are mourned, not just those caused by death, and we must allow our friends and loved ones freedom to mourn and have sympathy for their grief.

One final note: as an ordained Christian minister I cannot have been involved in grief work for over fourteen years without having heard the question, "Why, God?" asked thousands of times in the midst of suffering.

Therefore, toward the end of this book you will find a chapter entitled, Ongoing Thoughts About God and Suffering. This chapter is not an attempt to proselytize or to provide answers. It is, for the most part, simply a journal of my own ongoing and unfinished thoughts as I wrestle with one of the most painful aspects of mourning.

3

The Mourning Process

THE FIRST AND most important thing to remember when trying to help an adult friend in mourning is that that person needs you.

He may not know at a conscious level that he needs you.

He may not need you at *that particular moment*.

He may not need *you* at that particular moment.

And, for a long time he may need only a part of you at any given time.

But remember most of all that your adult friend in mourning needs you.

Before you try to help a friend in mourning, however, you should be aware that you may resent the intrusion of what has happened to him into your relationship. You may not want to admit that, but it is normal; and you aren't a bad or selfish or unthinking person for feeling it.

After all, something has changed. Future plans may be disrupted or even cancelled. A source of *sharing* will be cut off for perhaps a long time. And things will become terribly lopsided in your relationship. You are about to put yourself on the giving end for what may be a very long time to come.

Before you try to help a friend in mourning, just know that all this can happen, and that you may resent it from time to time. And know, too, that that is normal.

The person in mourning is no longer functioning as before. The equilibrium of his days and nights and consequently the equilibrium of any relationship the two of you have had no longer exists. It is gone.

And when an equilibrium does return many moons hence, it will not be the *same* equilibrium. Nothing will ever be *exactly* the same again. But an equilibrium of living, in all but the most severe situations, will return. And you can help.

Following is a discussion of the areas of mourning I have called Shock, including denial and numbness; Hurt, with acute pain and hollow ache; and Healing, reaching new equilibrium and integration.

As I have pointed out before, not everyone in mourning will progress through shock, hurt, and healing in definable order. And some people in mourning may experience reactions other than those named.

But being able to recognize the components of shock, hurt, and healing as mourning responses that can be *normal* can help those of us who are trying to be a friend to someone in mourning.

SHOCK

Shock is described by Dr. Kubler-Ross as the first stage of the dying person's response to news of his terminal condition. It is also the mourner's first response to death.

Initial shock comes in the form of *denial*. This is followed by shock in the form of *numbness*. The length of each phase of shock varies according to the manner of death, the relationship to the dead person, and the personality of the individual mourner. But no matter how expected the death was, shock, in the form of denial and numbness, is almost always the first response.

DENIAL

Denial shock usually is verbalized, "No!" This means: "No, it can't be true"; "No, I don't believe it"; "No, not *now*"; and, "No, don't do this to me—*I* can't take it. *I'm* not ready."

The death of someone we love is a horrible fact. To want to deny it, to pretend it could not be, is very normal. To take it personally is also very normal. When the phone call came, not only could I not believe Chris had died, but also, in those first moments when I heard the news, I had the sense that I had been violated. I had the strange sensation that a part of me had been beaten, cut away, dealt havoc with, mutilated, violated. And, in fact, that is just what had happened.

When Chris died, we were at a stage in our relationship when he was becoming a part of me, of my life, of who I was, of my daily identity. And the woman at the other end of the telephone line told me he was dead. Therefore, a part of *me*, a part of *my* identity, had been stolen away, had been "killed." My feeling of violation was based on fact.

And this feeling of violation was in great measure what led to my sensation of anger at Chris the next day. It was Chris after all who had died. And it was his death that left me feeling violated. So he must be the one responsible. He must be the one at whom I should be angry.

That, of course, was not rational. Rationally, if I had to be angry at the cause of my suffering, it would have been at the heart attack. The heart attack killed Chris. Chris didn't kill Chris.

But that, again, is the point—it is *normal* to react irrationally to an event as irrational, as "crazy," and as irrevocable as death. Thus, my sense of anger at Chris rather than at the heart attack that killed him was a normal reaction. But usually the person experiencing such anger is reluctant to discuss it, or even to admit it to himself at a conscious level, because it's not "nice" and surely it must not be normal to feel such unpleasant things at such a time.

A side note here: *Feeling* anger at a loved one for dying can be a normal mourning reaction. But the anger I directed at Chris that Saturday morning was not yet even a feeling, because I was still in shock. People in shock *cannot feel* anything emotionally or even, at times, physically. This is important to remember.

I remember the first time I experienced the death of a child. I was a student chaplain, and a baby had died while I was on call the night before. The following morning our supervisor kept trying to make me describe how I *felt* about the experience. I could describe the data, the "what happened." But I could not perform as otherwise requested. I could not describe how I felt. I didn't know then that I was still in shock and that a person in shock cannot feel, let alone describe feeling.

This *inability to feel as part of shock* is initially a protection. If it is sustained in the period preceding the funeral, it may enable the mourner to get through picking a casket, paying the morticians, standing about at the wake, and functioning through the burial with relative ease. But observers may find such competence in the face of death unnerving. Granger Westburg writes, "Sometimes at the funeral home we see the sorrowing wife and find that she is almost radiant as she greets those who come to offer their sympathy . . . the truth of the matter may well be that this woman is experiencing a temporary anesthesia. . . ."[1] Just as we have no feeling with anesthesia, so it is with shock.

And so, it is important to remember that *you can help a friend in the denial phase of shock by listening to him, but he probably won't tell you anything of substance about how he is feeling*. If he talks much at all in this stage, what he will be doing is trying to process the death information—the death data—as fact. You may hear much information, much retelling or reliving of experiences surrounding the death, and much repetition of the above. But you will probably hear little, if anything, about how your friend in mourning is feeling. And it really won't help him *at this time* to ask how he's feeling. Because he isn't.

How, then, can one best listen to someone talking through the denial phase of shock?

The two most important factors of Jane's and Jennifer's listening that Friday night Chris died were: 1) they let me know that they had *time* to listen and wanted to listen; and, 2) they listened. If you simply do not have time to listen at the moment you are asked, tell the person so. Emphasize that what he is experiencing is too momentous to be dealt with quickly; and that you do want to hear what happened in detail as soon as you can. Assure the person that you'll call back at the first opportunity and suggest several people he may call upon to meet his immediate need. Sometimes that is the most you can offer.

I was fortunate that night with Jane and Jennifer. Jane, having lost her daughter not long before, could certainly have been expected to interrupt with data concerning her child's death. On that strange continuum of "acceptable" deaths, her loss certainly was worse: Little Ryan Mile's two-year battle with a brain tumor and two-week pain-wrought suffering at the end versus Chris's one-day illness and quick death at age fifty.

But Jane did not interrupt with her story. This was *my time*—my mourning, my shock, my death experience; and she respected my credibility as a mourner, without need to quantify.

Jennifer works daily in the pediatric neurosurgery unit where Jane's daughter died, and where I, too, once studied chaplaincy. She also could have interrupted with scores of pathetic stories of ill and dying children she had grown to love. But she didn't. Jennifer also gave me my time and my credibility.

In listening to a friend in the shock of mourning you *never* can make him feel better by relating a "worse" experience, either your own or one you know about.

You also can *never* make a person in the shock of mourning feel better by saying, "I know how you feel"—even if you have a valid reason to believe you do know how the person feels. Later in the mourning process, it can be helpful to some mourners if you share feelings or data about a similar death experience you have had. *But only when asked or given an opening to do so by the mourner.*

Someone just learning of the death of one he loves may reach out to you *instinctively* because there is reason to think you can identify with him in his loss. I called my friend Jane first, I'm sure, because of what she and her family had been through with Ryan. But I did not call her because I thought she would know how *I* felt; rather because I knew instinctively that she would know what *it*—the "death experience"—feels like. Jane didn't say to me, "I know how you feel," because she didn't. She did know what *it* felt like to have to talk to someone at 11:30 at night because someone you love has died.

As mentioned earlier, it is important to remember that a person in mourning needs you, but that for a long time he will need only a *part* of you at any given time. And conversely, the person in mourning will be sharing only a small part of himself with you at any given time—*though he will perceive he is sharing all of himself with you.*

When I called Jane and Jennifer, I had an instinct that their understanding of the "death experience" would make them good listeners. But once they were on the phone and did indeed listen, they ceased to be Jane and Jennifer. They became ears for my voice. The part of Jane and Jennifer that I needed was their ears. The part of me that I shared was my voice—and that, at the time, was *all of me*. Because nothing else was functioning.

This sounds very cold, but it is true. Your friend in mourning—though he doesn't perceive himself that way—is self-centered. You simply cannot exist for him as a whole person, probably for a very long time. This can be hard on relationships. Friends get weary of ceasing to be perceived as human beings with feelings and problems and hopes in their own right. They get weary of being there for the other person in a seemingly one-sided relationship. But suffice it to say that your friend in mourning will not be able to empathize with you about things involving you for many months—or maybe years.

So to summarize: One of the best things you can do to help a friend in shock denial is simply to listen to his story, without inserting your own experiences or without reminding him that he is repeating himself or not making sense. There is a marvelous quote to this effect by Doug Manning. "The ear is the most powerful part of the human body. People are healed by the laying on of ears."[2]

NUMBNESS

Once shock denial progresses to *shock numbness*, your friend won't talk much. This is confusing for those who, until now, have been listening; but your friend in mourning will give clues to his needs. The best things you can offer your friend when his shock denial turns to shock numbness are "being with"—offering quiet presence, a hand to hold or a strong hug—and "doing."

For me, shock denial turned to shock numbness the instant I first saw Chris in his open casket. And that is the way it happens for many people. One can no longer intellectually deny the fact that a person is dead when he sees that person's body, especially full view, in an open casket.

A word here about "viewing" the body. Almost all writers on matters of death and dying stress the importance, for reality testing, of seeing the body of the person who has died. I agree completely with this and add that it is even more helpful to see the person's body at a mortuary. There are several reasons for this.

The mortuary is where dead bodies are taken. For many, the smell is unmistakable, the lighting seems ghostly, and the decor feels draped, cushioned, and claustrophobic. (Many funeral directors today are taking forward steps to change this image as well as to provide a variety of more comfortable situations for good-bye—saying by family and close friends. These funeral directors should be applauded and encouraged in their humane efforts.) All our lives we identify mortuaries and funeral homes with death. On the other hand, we do not necessarily identify hospitals, nursing homes, our own homes, scenes of accidents, and ambulances with death. To see the body in the mortuary, the house of death, so to speak, can therefore help seal the fact, the reality of the death. Even if the death had long been expected, denial may be operative, and a mortuary can move the mourners past that first stage of shock.

And following *sudden death*, seeing the body in a funeral home is truly vital. Seeing Chris in his flag-draped coffin was the first time I really accepted—intellectually—the fact that he was dead.

Chris did not die a violent death, and an open casket presented no problems for the mortician. In cases of violent death, however, open caskets can be difficult or impossible. Viewing the body is not done in order to see what damage death has wrought. If mutilation is such that no part of the body can be made presentable, then the body should not be viewed. When the casket must be closed, perhaps a lock of hair could be offered to mourners. (If the mortician doesn't offer such a keepsake, perhaps you as a friend could quietly check whether that would be a possibility. It could become precious in the mourning process and beyond.)

But even if only a small portion of the body can be made acceptable for a private viewing—with mourners warned *in some detail* beforehand what to expect—it will help greatly in their mourning process if a viewing can occur. This can happen before the wake or burial, if the casket is to be otherwise closed or if cremation is to take place.

Having private *time* with the person's body, either at the place of death or the mortuary, is also very helpful to many people. For reality testing—accepting the fact of death—seeing the body in a mortuary is best. But for saying good-byes, touching and holding the person's body, private time at the place or time of death is best since the body likely will still be warm and flexible.

Regardless of the place, however, seeing the dead person's body and having some private time, if desired, is very important for accepting the reality of death and saying good-bye. (As a friend, this may be another way you can help. You may be in a position to arrange some private viewing time for your friend to be with the body of the person she loves, and accompany her to or from the site. In the confusion of things at the time of death this can be overlooked if not offered to mourners by hospital or mortuary staff, or arranged by a member of the clergy.

Seeing Chris in his casket, I had to admit in my mind that he was dead. Seeing his hard-clenched hands and touching his sleeve which crinkled like wrapping paper, I knew, in fact, that he was dead. *But knowing someone is dead and believing someone is dead are two different things.* Herein lies the beginning of *numb shock.*

As described earlier, the moment I saw Chris in his coffin my body went numb and I couldn't talk beyond a word or two. Yes, seeing Chris in his casket, I now *knew* he was dead. But I still was not ready to *believe* that he was dead. And, therefore, *I no longer wanted to talk about Chris's death. Because if I talked about it I risked talking myself into believing it, or letting others talk me into believing it.*

And until I believed he was dead I didn't have to act on that belief. In this situation, acting on the belief that Chris was dead meant feeling, allowing myself to feel. *And that feeling would be pain.* Who wants to feel pain? So I went numb, and could not talk beyond a word or two.

In denial shock I did not feel because I could not feel. In numb shock I did not feel because I was afraid to feel, afraid of the pain that would come with believing.

Numb shock—*knowing* intellectually that someone we love has died, but resisting believing he has died—not only means not discussing the death, it means a number of other "nots": Not sleeping, at least with any regularity, for the numb body is neither tired nor awake; not eating with any regularity, for the numb body is neither hungry nor full; not hearing phones or doorbells; not seeing floral tributes; and not reading or absorbing sympathy notes, for something that is not yet believed cannot be taken to heart.

And herein lies the main reason we are prevented from truly comforting someone in the shock of mourning: Hurt from a known fact that is not yet believed cannot be soothed. Feelings that one is fighting desperately not to feel, for fear of their magnitude, cannot be gotten out.

It is hard to do anything for a person in *shock denial* but listen.

But listening at the *shock numbness* stage is virtually impossible because mourners at this stage won't talk. They know that if they talk they'll have to focus on what they want most of all to avoid: believing the fact that someone they love is dead.

How, then, in addition to quiet presence, a held hand or a warm hug, can we help the person who has gone from shock denial to shock numbness?

The person in numb shock is very malleable, almost like a puppet. Left to his own devices, he will sit for long periods of time, simply staring. He will move from place to place in his own world, with his own agenda, which may or may not have any rationality to it. His reflex actions will be dull. He will be more clumsy and accident-prone. His movement and speech will be slower. He will probably be only vaguely aware of his own movements or the movements of others. He may have little or no concept of time; for he has needed to stop the world; and if he is at all aware that it is still going on, he is resentful of that fact and fighting desperately to turn back the clock.

But it can be at just this time of numbness—the numbness that resists all attempts to invade it—that the person in mourning will have to make a number of important decisions and perform a number of complicated tasks.

You can never be all things to a friend in mourning, or at any other time. And you shouldn't try. However, you can probably think of several things which may be helpful at this time, whether to do yourself or to cause to be done. I will list some suggestions as a guide, but there are many more than I can think of or have space for.

As mentioned earlier, you may be able to arrange a quiet time with the body for family or friends. You could also: answer the telephone and the doorbell; make sure all sympathy cards and flower tags are kept in one place; note the kind of flower on the back of the flower tag and put the address of the sender there, too, if it is known. You can help select clothing for your friend to wear to the wake and the funeral, you can do laundry, clean, wash floors, polish shoes, do dishes, vacuum, chauffeur, find a photograph or other information a newspaper may need, cook, or arrange for child care if needed.

There is a wonderful story about a man who arrived at the home of a friend in mourning and said, ''I have come to polish your shoes,'' and did. It was something that was greatly appreciated by all those who had to dress for the wake and funeral.

You can place floral arrangements. You can make necessary plane or other transportation arrangements, or meet people at points of arrival. You can see to urgent mail or make hotel reservations. You can grocery shop, fill in with the car pool, call employers, cancel plans that need to be cancelled.

You might consider what groups the mourner belongs to and notify them. These may be religious, social, or business groups. Others in those groups may wish to help, and if so you can start entrusting responsibilities, thus ensuring that offers of help are put to use over a sustained period of time. A little organization can go a long way toward seeing that your friend receives the help he needs not just in the first days, but the first weeks or even months of mourning.

One area in which you may be helpful is in helping to plan the funeral service. Some faiths have standard services which must be adhered to by all. If this is so with your friend, the traditional service will likely bring comfort as it is. However, even in those circumstances there may be a priest, minister, or rabbi who is particularly close to the family and could help to make the service more special and more personal simply by his or her participation. Try to determine your friend's wishes if you are close enough and if you feel this has not been thought of. Take care, however, not to cause family friction. Move quietly and cautiously.

If there is flexibility allowed, and if your friend desires, helping him personalize the service could be a great relief at this time. Especially in cases of sudden death, when burial services have not been thought about ahead of time, your friend may not know where to begin. You could help him provide some details that will not only personalize the standard text but will be of comfort to him and other close family members and friends.

I myself find burial services which honor the special, individual qualities of the dead person particularly meaningful. If this is allowed in your friend's faith, you could help by gathering materials and calling people your friend would like to participate. As with informing people of the actual death, this last may be something your friend or other family members wish to do themselves. You should ask permission to become involved in such personal matters. But do not *assume* your involvement isn't wanted. And don't assume someone else is doing what needs to be done. Often that is not the case, and often it is greatly helpful to a family to have assistance from one or more caring friends who are not in the immediate throes of mourning.

Whatever you do, it is important to do it with as little fanfare as possible. Things will be confusing enough; and the quieter you can be as you go about your task—without engaging in morbid whispers—the better. If your friend talks, listen. If he doesn't, don't feel you need to carry on a monologue. Also, it is not necessary to keep asking permission (as it is with personal matters) to answer a doorbell or a phone each time it rings—just do so. When you arrive you can simply say to your friend, "I'm here to help in whatever way I can unless that is not something you want right now." You may get only a nod or smile in return, but it will mean yes, please stay.

If you are *not* needed at that time, however, your friend almost always will say so. If that happens, take your cue and leave. Don't be hurt or offended. You have tried, but the time was not right. A time *will come* that will be right, *so don't give up*. I repeat: the person in mourning needs you; but he may not need *you* at that particular moment; he may not need you *at that particular moment*, and for a long time he will need only a part of you at any given time.

You still can go home and cook something to send to the house. You can write a sympathy note, or arrange for masses to be said, or use that time to store up energy for when you will be needed. Because most likely that time will come.

It is a rare, and ill, person who can ignore forever the *belief* that one he loves has died. Shock may last a long time, but *belief must come in order for true mourning and healing to begin*. For me, belief began to win at Chris's funeral.

When I arrived at the funeral service, I was still in numb shock. I was still fighting with everything inside me not to believe that Chris was dead. I had this feeling of building pressure, of wanting everyone to stay clear of me, to not say a word to me.

As I stood in the outer alcove of the church not wanting to go in, I remember vividly seeing a girl who had resigned from our office to await the birth of her first child. The very pregnant woman came up to me and started to talk. She wanted to know the details of Chris's death, exactly when and how, and how the people at the office were taking it. These were all normal questions, especially since she had not known that Chris and I dated. But rather than tell her I just didn't feel like talking then, which would have been kinder, I simply nodded to her first few sentences, looked the other way, and then retreated into the church, into a pew by myself, having said nothing beyond "hello." I remembered she looked hurt and surprised.

Later, when I was able to comprehend my actions, I was sorry for my rudeness. But at the time I couldn't do other than I did. Having moved from the denial phase of shock, where I talked about the death to establish fact, into the numb phase of shock, where I desperately fought believing the fact, I simply *could not* talk. I couldn't risk letting myself believe what I knew intellectually, even enough to be polite. I didn't know it then, but the grenade pin was about to be pulled. I was about to lose the battle. I was about to *have to believe* that Chris was dead. And worse, I was about to have to *feel*; about to have to *feel pain*.

HURT

Just as there is *no* feeling in the shock response to death, there is an immense amount of feeling when belief finally comes and actual mourning begins. The nature of this feeling is violent, racking pain at first, not only emotional pain, but often physical pain as well.

Being very strong-willed, or as some would say "hardheaded," I tried to wall myself up against this pain for as long as possible when Chris died. When I deserted my pregnant friend and fled into the pew in the back of the old Catholic church, I was still fighting with every ounce of strength in me to remain numb.

Finally the pressure inside me was so intense that release had to come. I wanted to scream—which would have been therapeutic, but was impossible in the church setting. I also felt as though I wanted to beat my head against the wall. (It is safer, when you subconsciously know you have to feel, to feel something from the outside rather than risk feeling what is inside.) And although therapeutic if one has a padded wall, that, too was impossible in the church setting.

So I cried, not with sobs—for I was still fighting feeling by trying to "stay together" while with people, in church—but with steady, silent tears, like a heavy rain washing down a window-pane. That much feeling I simply could no longer contain.

The tears came suddenly, without warning, and for a time I could *not* stop them, no matter how hard I tried. Finally, enough tears came that I was able to experience some release and I could take control enough to exit the church, find Jennifer's car, and take my place in the procession. I remember several friends from work strongly suggesting that I ride with them to the cemetery. But I sensed I could not hold on to my numbness with other people around. I could not be with anyone, for fear of letting go again.

But, in fact, when I climbed into Jennifer's trusty, old, frog-green car by myself, I had entered a no-man's-land. I was neither dead nor alive, not feeling or totally unfeeling. I was squarely between the numbness of denial and the hurt of belief. *If this limbo persists indefinitely, there can be serious emotional handicaps.*

Fortunately, for most people faced with the fact of death, disbelief eventually gives way to belief, numbness to feeling. We protect ourselves with shock as long as it is necessary. Then, when we can begin, with hesitant, halting steps, to handle the tragedy, our minds protect us from insanity by pushing us forward into feeling and reality. This is a *normal* process, with varying time frames. And when it is inhibited or suppressed, long-term damage is possible.

The initial steps of belief are fleeting. Disbelief and belief play leapfrog with each other for a long time because the first pain of belief is so devastating and violent. But when that feeling of pain does come the person is taking his first steps into the long healing process of mourning. And, as healing often is, it is a painful process.

My no-man's-land, the time of neither feeling or not feeling, of fighting to regain numbness after the first crack had appeared in the wall I'd put up against reality, came to an explosive end as I was driving to the cemetery. It came in that split second when I pictured Chris's bony knee and *knew* I would never pound on it again. That mental image was so powerful that it crashed headlong through my numbness into my whole being. The wall between fact and belief collapsed. I *believed* Chris was dead. From dead as a *word*, to dead as a *fact*, to dead as a *belief*. The denial of shock to the numbness of shock to the pain of belief: *Chris truly is dead.*

My tears had no boundaries; their force consumed my body. Only by instinct and the help of the slow-moving funeral procession was I saved from an accident. I was unable to see, convulsed in sobs for mile upon mile. It was a pain that was just beginning.

The beginning of feeling is the beginning of true mourning, and it leads inevitably to an onslaught of sensations: physical and emotional pain, tears, screams, rage, guilt, fear, the "crazies," questioning, deep sighs, and emptiness—all competing with each other daily, sometimes hourly, consuming the person in the act of mourning.

In the beginning, when the pain of feeling becomes too severe, the mourner will very likely try to ease it by trying to return to the numbness of shock. Not able to do this, he simply stops his world.

In time, as the intensity of acute pain lessens, the long-term ache of mourning begins and he engages in deep sighing and mental wrestling about the value of life. His ability to think rationally slowly returns. And when it does, it is inevitable that the mourner questions the value of life in the face of the absurdity of death.

And pondering that question can, strangely, make breathing itself laborious. Thus come the deep audible sighs that issue from feelings of meaninglessness and hopelessness. In looking at this complex phase of mourning I have called "Hurt," it may be easier to break it down into parts, the first of which is pain.

ACUTE PAIN

Pain in mourning can be physical as well as emotional. The sense of violation that I had when I was in shock became a cramping pain in my stomach when I began to feel. It hurt more to sit up straight, less to sit slightly bent, holding my stomach. I became aware of a heaviness in my arms and legs. My back hurt, and I was terribly tired whether or not I had slept. I had headaches, and I developed a mild case of ulcerative colitis.

All of these physical symptoms and others can be *normal* in the process of mourning. Often in our lives true physical illness results from emotional distress.

Some people in mourning may have no physical symptoms, though that is rare. Others may have symptoms different from mine. But in most situations some form of physical distress is usual and normal in the mourning process. The severity will differ greatly from case to case: some people may require the treatment of a physician; others can be treated with over-the-counter medications.

The other form of pain that comes during mourning is emotional pain. This is very complicated, cannot be treated with an aspirin, and will not go away in a few hours or days. It remains in many forms and degrees for a long time.

Emotional pain can be dulled by medication. But most professionals working in the area of death and dying are adamantly against the use of these suppressants, such as Valium or Librium. I agree completely. *Suppressants hinder the mourning process rather than help it.* Taking Valium at moments of extreme anguish in the days immediately following a death can, I suppose, be helpful. But an open prescription or full bottle of the drug is a mistake. It is going to be hell, this time of mourning, and dulling the senses won't take away the truth—but it could suppress normal and necessary stages in grieving.

Emotional pain is expressed in a number of ways: tears, anger, guilt, and fear. When these threaten to overwhelm, that's when the "crazies" come in. Some "crazies" put a momentary end to pain.

Fear, guilt, and anger are very closely linked in the mourning process and it is extremely difficult to separate them. They may enter the mind all but simultaneously, and thereupon remain inextricable.

As an example: John and Mary were driving to a party and they were sideswiped by a hit-and-run driver. John was killed; Mary shaken but uninjured. During the mourning process, Mary may fear that she will not be able to survive in body or soul without John. She may become angry at the driver, angry at the senselessness of the situation, and angry at God for not protecting them. And she may feel guilty for her anger at God; guilty that she was the one responsible for their being out in the car; guilty that she was the one who was spared; and/or guilty that she hadn't loved John more. One thought leads swiftly to another. And often the periods of anger or guilt or fear in the mourning process are only vaguely definable.

How, then, can one be a friend to a person going through the pain of mourning?

The first thing to remember is that all these feelings of pain, both physical and emotional, are normal. The person is not losing her mind, or falling apart, even if she appears to be. In fear, anger, or guilt, your friend may often confuse rational and irrational reactions. But both are normal.

Being there, and again being available for listening, are paramount for the person who is trying to help. But you must be there and be open to listening while still remembering that no one person can be all things to a person in mourning. It is all right to say, "No" when listening or being with is impossible or a real hardship. By saying "No" today you can have the energy and patience to say "Yes" another time. The important thing is to keep a line of communication open, something less difficult in the pain phase of hurt, and far more difficult in the long ache phase of hurt.

Pain expressed as fear is one logical response of the mourner uncertain of how her day-to-day living needs will be met in the future. From infancy on we have a normal fear of not having our basic living needs met. A person in mourning often will not express this fear verbally so as not to appear crass or mercenary. But the fear can be very real and can add a heavy weight to an already heavy emotional burden.

Immediate help with food, transportation, child care, cleaning, etc. will be greatly appreciated at such a time. But the person's fear usually is for more long-term needs.

If you have resources to offer, this can be the time to say so. "If you need anything financially, Mary, to help tide you over, I want you to know that I am able to help." When saying something like this, do it out of earshot of others. Touch her, take her hand or shoulder, and look at her in the eye. This is optimal communication and rarely will be brushed aside if the need is there. And if there is no need, the firm communication of understanding and support will still be greatly appreciated as a sign of caring.

If you cannot help financially but are able to intercede with persons or institutions who might, then offer to do so. This too will be appreciated.

Fear of the future is not only a basic "needs" fear. It can be fear of vulnerability, of aloneness, of emptiness, of overwhelming daily burdens, of changes in patterns of living, of not being touched, or of never having someone to be that intimate with again.

These fears often remain below the surface during the initial pain of loss, so they manifest themselves in less rational, but also normal, patterns such as some of those described below.

A person may fear that she, too, will die. Feelings of vulnerability creep in—if it can happen to someone this close to me, it can happen to me.

A person may fear living on without her loved one. Passing thoughts, and occasionally even plans of suicide, are not uncommon at this time. The overwhelming presence of death can make it seem like the only act in town. Death and mental pictures of the dead person permeate many waking and sleeping hours. Death can seem to be the only way to be with the loved one or to ease the pain of mourning.

In her poignant and excellent book, *The Grieving Time*, Anne Brooks describes how thoughts of suicide stuck in her mind the first few months after her husband's death.

". . . I do believe he is somewhere. That belief is the thin thread that holds my sanity, the thought that perhaps someday, somehow, I will be with him again. This is half the magnetism drawing me to suicide; the other half is simply that life is too unbearable without him."[3]

Thoughts of suicide can enter the mourning process in an even more irrational way. In the mourner's mind's eye, the person who died still retains feeling; and that person is out there alone, frightened, cold, claustrophobic, and feeling forgotten and unloved. The mourner feels that she should die to be with the dead person, to protect him or share these feelings with him, to let the dead person know that he is not alone.

I didn't think of suicide when Chris died, but I acted out my concern for him as part of my "crazies": putting the paper kiss in the grave for Chris to "find" and literally sitting with him so he would feel at home and not forgotten for over four hours the first day he was in his grave. My hurt and fear at losing Chris were so overpowering that I simply could *not* lose him. I went to be with him, as if he would know and feel that I was there.

The thought of suicide didn't enter my mind, perhaps because of the limited length and nature of our relationship, or perhaps because the "crazies" allowed me to act out my protective instincts toward Chris, my longing to be with him, without taking them to the extreme of wanting to be with Chris in death. When the pain and fear became too great and I couldn't return to numbness, I simply stopped my world and went crazy *in order to remain sane.* I stopped everything to do with living and went to be with Chris.

Along with the "crazies" (which will be discussed in greater detail later), there are other overwhelming reactions such as anger and guilt, which fight for our attention during this time of great pain. All of these usually serve to overpower, with their agendas, any thoughts of suicide before they can take a firm hold.

You can be most helpful to your friend in fearful, pain-filled mourning by listening to his fears without being judgmental, without telling him his fears are baseless, without suggesting that his love can be replaced, without being horrified if he mentions suicide, and without trying to cajole him into changing the subject.

When you do talk, it is important to reassure your friend that the fears he has are a normal part of the mourning process. Fears of our vulnerability to death are normal when thoughts of death are uppermost in our minds. It is normal to project loneliness and visions of permanent unfulfillment onto the future when we begin to believe in the death of someone we love, normal to want to die as an escape from that bleak future, normal to want to continue to be with that person.

Well-meaning friends wanting to help a person through fear, or guilt, or sometimes anger in mourning, will try to cajole the person out of those real feelings by minimizing them and telling the person he has no reason to feel that way. This makes the mourner feel he is abnormal and that there is something wrong with him; so he ceases to talk about his fears and guilts and angers. But they don't go away. They only compound inside him. And because he has no release for them, his natural mourning process may be blocked; serious, long-term emotional damage can result. It is important to help your friend express his feelings of fear, guilt, and anger and let him know that it is *normal* to have such feelings when in mourning.

Guilt is particularly common in mourning. A person will feel guilty that he, by commission or omission, caused the death of the person he loves. "If only I had called the doctor sooner."

"If only I hadn't forced him to go to that party." "If only I had loved him more."

The person who is mourning after a long-term dying experience may have experienced some of these guilts during his loved one's dying process; but, regardless, they will return now, though likely for a shorter time.

As long as you let your friend talk these guilts out you are helping him. At first he may simply repeat the "if onlys" or the "whys" over and over again, without being ready for you to speak, or without being ready to help himself reason things through. The pain of guilt is horrendous. But the mourner may, in a strange way, *need* to feel that pain. He may subconsciously think that since the person he loved suffered the pain of death, he, the mourner, must somehow feel pain and suffer, too. To flog oneself with guilt is one way of inflicting pain.

Eventually, the time will come when reason can enter the picture. But helping the person reason out his guilts does not mean these guilts will magically disappear. The "if onlys" and "whys" will return. They may return with less frequency and intensity, but they will return, perhaps for years.

As an example of helping the mourner reason out his guilts, let's return to the story of John and Mary, whose car was sideswiped by the hit-and-run driver. Mary felt guilty that she was angry with God; guilty that she was the one who was spared; guilty that she was the reason they were out that night at all, and guilty that she had not loved John more.

"Why did I drag John to that party? If only we had stayed home this would never have happened."

There is, of course, no way that Mary could have foreseen that this would happen. But rather than saying, "Mary, there's no way you could have known this," the friend can help her try to reason it out for herself.

Friend: "Did you know this was going to happen when you decided to go to the party?"

Mary: "Of course not."

Friend: "Is there any way you could have known this was going to happen before you went to the party?"

Mary: "No."

Friend: "If you had known that this would happen if you went, would you still have gone?"

Mary: "No!" By now Mary is probably beginning to wonder if you're crazy, which is all to the good.

But rather than continue with this line of questioning the friend may simply say, "Mary, feeling guilty in a situation like this is normal. If it happened to my husband and me I'm sure I would have feelings of guilt, too. Our husbands are always trying to make us feel we are dragging them to parties—until they get there and have a good time! It's part of the 'husband's job description.'

"But you and I know that you didn't want to go to that party badly enough to exchange John's life for it. That is a fact. And we also know that you could not have foreseen that this would happen or you wouldn't have gone. That too is fact.

"Saying 'if only' and asking 'why' are *normal* reactions, but they're not rational. You can beat yourself into the ground for years with this guilt, but if the situation were reversed, and you had died, would you want John to do this?"

This is an example of a way to help someone, when the time is right, begin to reason through his pain of guilt in mourning. Mary won't be able to process or accept all of that as it's being said. But, as the acuteness of the pain lessens, she will reach a point where she will be able to use bits and pieces of that conversation to reinforce her slowly returning rational feelings, even though her "if onlys" and "whys" will crop up occasionally again and again for a long time.

Similar help can be given in reasoning out the mourner's guilt that he is the one who survived. Helping a person reason through, step by step, that those things are beyond our control and that he was not given the choice of who should die will reinforce for the mourner that these feelings, too, are normal but not rational.

As far as the feeling of guilt that she could have loved John more, Mary could not be more normal. Almost everyone, no matter how beautiful their love, wishes at the time of death that they could have loved more, loved better. Help your friend know this, too, is normal. Giving the mourner an example of some instance in which the dead person spoke to you lovingly about him can be of great help, reassuring him that *he* made his loved one feel loved, and that that person spoke openly of that feeling to others. This can help especially if it was an instance of which the mourner knew nothing.

If, by chance, the mourner's guilt is based on medical questions, you can help by encouraging your friend to discuss the issue with the physician involved.

Perhaps Mary was haunted by the question that once she had regained consciousness, had she been able to make it to a telephone to call an ambulance her husband might have been saved. The best therapy for Mary would be the physician, the person with the degree, saying to her, "Mrs. Smith, there was nothing you could have done. Time, in your husband's case, would not have mattered. He died instantly, there was no pain."

The physician's addition of "no pain" is also very helpful. Mary's haunting mental picture may have been of her husband lying there suffering a slow and painful death, and she may never have had the opportunity to have those fears spoken to by the attending physician.

Some hospitals now have programs in which families of people who died in the emergency room or were dead on arrival are given the chance, several weeks after the death, to ask questions about the death either through a visit to the hospital or through a phone call. This is immeasurably helpful in integrating reality into the process of death and in alleviating the horror movies that endlessly replay themselves in the mourner's mind.

Mourners can always find something to feel guilty about, but whether they focus on sins of omission or commission, their guilt is rarely founded in fact. One can help a friend by letting him talk about these guilts, as with his fears, without being judgmental; without telling him immediately that his guilt is baseless; without making him feel abnormal; and without trying to cajole him away from the topic by denying the power and validity of his feelings. Once he has talked about these guilts several times, or for a long time, you can then, in a quiet and private setting, start to introduce some reality and help your friend reason through them.

There are, of course, situations in which a person's guilt involving the death of someone he loves is founded in fact. And there also are situations when a loved one does not "die instantly," but suffers great and prolonged pain even though death is inevitable.

In the first instance, professional therapy is often needed to help the mourner work through his guilt. If punishment by law is appropriate, this can help somewhat, in a strange way, because it can be viewed as official public atonement. But usually legal punishment in and of itself is not enough.

You can be a friend to your friend feeling justifiably guilty by listening, by agreeing without judgment that his guilt is in fact rational, by suggesting he seek professional therapy, and by helping him direct his "atonement" into positive action to benefit others rather than continuing to flog himself—and perhaps ruin his own life. The adage "two wrongs don't make a right" is valid. Two wasted lives don't make a salvaged life.

Wherein a loved one suffered great pain in the minutes or hours before death and nothing was done to alleviate the pain, it is unlikely a physician will tell a mourner so. The chances of a similar situation recurring later are extremely remote. The physician would not want the mourner to suffer even more by telling him that there was something he *could* have done. Other than any later applicable "lesson" to be learned from the tragedy, a description of pain and suffering is cruel and cannot alter the fact. Most often, however, a victim in a fatal accident, for example, goes into shock and loses consciousness, thereby avoiding prolonged pain.

Fear, guilt, and anger are particularly common in mourning violent death. For death by violence, such as John's by a hit-and-run driver, or others by murder, suicide, or fire, for example, seem so preventable. The senselessness of violent death, as opposed to death from terminal illness, heart attack, etc., is magnified because with just a bit of prescience, or caution, or caring—as we endlessly remind ourselves—it seems as though death could have been avoided. Human error is so trivial, its consequences so momentous, that we are enraged and terrified by their juxtaposition in our lives.

When violent death occurs, whether at the hands of a deranged murderer or by self-infliction or because of unpredictable human circumstances, fear, guilt, and anger are often magnified in mourning. We keep trying to find a reason, and keep needing to place blame and, at times, to get revenge. It is a nightmare to know that someone you love was tortured, raped and murdered, gunned down, killed by his own hand, burned to death in a plane, drowned, or was a victim of any of the other forms of violent death that are possible. In trying to help a friend mourn a violent death, it often takes much talking on his part and much listening on yours before the mental horrors can even begin to fade.

Anger will permeate the conversation, but it is more than anger. It is fear that if it happened to him it could happen to me. It is guilt—whether of omission or commission. And it is rage at the senselessness of violent death, at the perpetrator of the "human failure" that caused the death, and possibly at a God perceived as absent or uncaring.

In violent death, the mourner's anger, guilt, need to gain revenge, or feelings of stigma may be so profound and intense that you can best be his friend by encouraging him to seek professional help.

In violent or "unusual" deaths the mourner can become fixated on one particular issue, such as guilt, and his mourning process can be inhibited. Or, the horror or stigma of the tragedy can be so great that the mourner will need more than friends and "less-affected" family to pull him through.

It is my strong recommendation that anyone whose loved one has died a violent or horror-filled or socially stigmatized death seek professional counseling or therapeutic group support to help him through the mourning process.

This does not mean you cannot still listen to your friend and "be there" with him. In fact, in deaths involving suicide or murder, often friends withdraw *because* of a sense of embarrassment or horror, so it is important to stay with your friend. But at the same time it is important to urge him to seek professional help and guidance through this "unfamiliar land" of mourning violent death.

Regardless of the nature of the death, however, the mourner will feel anger. If a person's dying was long-term, anger may have surfaced a number of times before the death: anger (unspoken, most likely) at the person for dying; anger at a nurse or technician or possibly, though more rarely, at the physician; anger at innocent bystanders; anger at medical science for its inadequacies; anger at the government for too many misdirected funds; anger at spouses, relatives, and friends; and anger at God.

Following the death, or in sudden death, many of the angers previously mentioned will appear, along with anger directed at all of the bureaucratic procedures related to death, like dealing with the funeral home, closing bank accounts, hearing the will, going through probate, and the thousand and one other necessary, but petty details that were not anticipated.

But anger is a feeling that wears itself out. It takes great energy to remain actively angry for a prolonged period of time. To listen to your friend's anger, as you may have listened to fear and guilt before, without judgment and without minimizing, will help more than anything to defuse this anger. Here you may have to do little reasoning with him; for in the heat of anger he won't want to reason. Once the anger is spent, your friend will weary of it and want to put it aside for a time. Slowly his anger will become less violent and appear less frequently. But anger will remain, at some level, as long or longer than his guilt, for there probably will be little if any meaningful retribution, regardless of the nature of the death.

At times people are able to feel a sense of retribution by turning their anger into accomplishment. Many Jews have done this, in response to the horror of the holocaust by building memorials to those lost. Mothers Against Drunk Drivers (MADD) have focused on winning legislative sanctions against those who caused their loved ones' deaths. This certainly is a positive way to deal with anger—but not one available to everyone.

Another positive way to deal with anger is to forgive. This is extremely difficult, if not impossible, for many people, especially in the pain of mourning. If your friend can *genuinely* forgive others involved—or himself—he can do much toward his healing. To try to do this before he truly can mean it, however, will be of little help.

Finally, what about tears? Tears are a release for the raw, cutting edges of pain. They are like a burst of cool water poured over hot metal. The water turns to steam and cools the surface, but inside the metal is still fiercely hot. And that is the important thing to remember: *tears alone will get no one through mourning.*

Do let your friend cry, but also give him permission to talk. Let him know that even though you understand his need to weep, you are also there for him to talk to about his feelings when he is able or has the need.

Weeping *with* your friend at times can help, too. It is sharing the only thing you can truly share surrounding the death: helplessness. You are helpless to give him what he wants, and he is helpless to effect what he wants—the return to life of the person he loves. Crying in the face of the real pain of helplessness can help you both.

Being there and being available to listen are very important in helping a friend through the pain of mourning. But if this is uncomfortable for you, you can also help by continuing the acts of "doing" that I described earlier in the section on Shock. The person in mourning is still extremely self- and death-oriented, and has often stopped his world in order to preserve sanity. Stopping the world is a good defense, but it does not get many daily needs attended to.

In summary, then, the things that can help greatly during this time of intense pain are: non-judgmental listening; being there; doing; and/or in time, helping a person reason through his guilts, angers, and fears with a willingness to hold a hand, give a hug, or lend a shoulder.

The Crazies

Finally, we have reached our discussion of the "crazies," which can keep us sane when the pain of mourning threatens to overpower us.

Believing the person is dead is the first step in the active mourning process. But having that belief, and acting on it day to day and minute to minute, can sometimes be more than anyone can bear. It is just too painful. So, to protect themselves from this pain, people in mourning will do all kinds of "crazy" things to try to hold on to the person who is dead.

I have described my kiss, my grave-sitting, and my journey to find flowers for Chris's grave. All of those were attempts to keep him—attempts to deny, for a time, the horrible and painful truth that he would not be alive in my life again. I did other odd things too—all of them normal for my situation of mourning; but certain to appear irrational, abnormal, "crazy," to anyone not in mourning.

Therefore, I didn't tell anyone about my "crazies" until, as mentioned earlier, I hesitantly introduced them in a speech I gave several years later. Then, and many times thereafter, they were validated by hundreds of other people who had had similar experiences that they, too, had rarely, if ever, admitted.

Before I continue to discuss my personal crazies in mourning Chris's death, a word of caution: normal mourning crazies can become abnormal if they persist for an extraordinary length of time or if they are used as a long-term escape from reality. The length and manner of normal mourning crazies vary so much from person to person that I hesitate to suggest limits. I will suggest that, for the most part, a person experiencing normal crazies knows at some level that he is doing something irrational. When a person begins to do these things without knowing that they are unusual or odd to him, then danger may exist.

Intellectually, I knew that Chris would not see the kiss I left in his empty grave, I knew I hated plastic flowers, and I knew sitting on Chris's grave for four and a half hours would not really help him. But I also knew I was *comfortable* doing each of these things. I had a *need* to do each of these things. They were necessary at the time for me to cope with the pain I then was feeling. Also, I did not pre-plan the kiss, the flowers, or the grave-sitting. They simply seemed natural things to do at the time.

The second time I grave-sat with Chris, I did so only three hours; that was enough. The third visit, less time was necessary. And soon I found that grave-sitting was no longer necessary to relieve my pain. I no longer needed to stop my world in that way, for that length of time. In total, that took about five weeks and four cemetery visits.

I also developed a very pronounced short-term memory loss that lasted two to three months, but it steadily improved during that time. The memory loss only dealt with current, day-to-day events; never with Chris or his death or anything that preceded it. This was yet another way to stop my world, by not attending to what was taking place in the present.

Two other bizarre, or "crazy," things I did during this time of pain were to notice every funeral home in the city, and to read all of the obituaries.

Before Chris died I drove by funeral homes without even seeing them. But for several months after his death I noticed every funeral home I passed.

And for several weeks or more, I made a daily practice of reading the obituaries. I would look only for gender and age. Any time I read of a man who died who was older than Chris I felt cheated. "See," I'd think, "that man lived to be sixty, or seventy or eighty. That's certainly more normal than dying suddenly at fifty." Or when I read of a man who died, especially suddenly, and was younger than Chris, I would think, "I know how those who love him feel—cheated. It's not fair."

After a while I didn't notice funeral homes again or read unknown people's obituaries. But even today, when I hear of a man fifty or under dying I think of Chris and how I felt. All of this, too, was an attempt to dwell on the dead and not the living, an attempt to stop the world at death.

Repetition is another way in which the crazies can keep the world at bay. After I didn't do it any longer, friends told me how much I had repeated myself in the months after Chris died. I hadn't realized it, and they had been sensitive enough not to mind or say anything at the time. It was easier for me to repeat things from the past that I associated with Chris's life and death than it was to incorporate new data from a forward-moving world. I wasn't ready for my world to move forward.

There are a number of other crazies—as many as there are mourners, no doubt. People sleep with a photo of their loved one pasted to a pillow; or with articles of his clothing wrapped around a pillow; or they sleep in articles of the dead person's clothing. These practices are especially normal for widows and widowers, and can continue for quite some time.

Perhaps you have read of people who leave all of the dead person's belongings—his room, his clothing, etc.—untouched, just as they were the last time the dead person was there. This is all right for a while, but if *all* time is stopped and the room is made into a perpetual shrine—the Miss Havisham syndrome of *Great Expectations*—it can be dangerous.

Keeping several special things is understandable and therapeutic. I still have Chris's goat, and though it is dusty and in a closet, I am still reluctant to part with it. But preserving everything as it was can be harmful to the mourner and to his progress toward healing.

However, it may be just as harmful to do the opposite. Some people try to run away, change jobs, sell homes, engage in casual sexual relationships, remarry immediately on the "rebound," or discard all of the dead person's belongings. However, they cannot run away from death. They will not be able to put an end to mourning by living or working in new surroundings, remarrying too soon, or immediately discarding the loved one's possessions. In fact, these or similar precipitous actions could impede the mourning process, with bad long-term effects.

A rule of thumb that most professionals offer is not to make *any* drastic life changes for at least one year. Altering the way holidays or vacations are spent can ease those hurtful times a bit, depending on the family situation. But it is wise to make no major changes in the first year, lest some of them prove difficult or impossible to undo if, as often happens in times of stress, a mistake has been made.

Both leaving the dead person's effects unchanged and making a complete clean sweep are attempts to stop the world at the point of death. And both are to be avoided.

When all is said and done, the pain of mourning is a horrible thing, but it is the only door through which healing can begin. Initial pain includes acute emotional and often physical distress. It includes tears and helplessness, and fear and anger and guilt, all of which can be so intense that a mourner may need to stop his world to endure, to act "crazy" for a time in order to remain sane.

I have mentioned ways to help a friend through tears, fear, anger, and guilt. To help a friend through the crazies one needs simply to *let him be crazy*. He might not mention why he is doing what he is doing, or even that he is doing it at all. But if he has called on you or allowed you to be with him to talk or cry, and then suddenly ceases to call, give him room. He may be grave-sitting, or talking to the dead person, or looking at albums, or lying in bed holding his pillow with a blouse of the dead person wrapped around it, or otherwise acting out the crazies. He may not want you to know that, not for a long time, if ever. Don't pry or make him feel guilty or abnormal; he is fighting for his sanity.

You can check up on your friend every now and then—a phone call or a drop-by without staying long if he seems vague. Eventually he'll come out of the crazies. He'll start and stop, start and stop, perhaps for a long while—longer than you may expect if you have not experienced a similar loss—until the intensity of acute pain subsides and the long-term ache begins. It is here that he must journey through a great abyss alone.

HOLLOW ACHE

I now do a great deal of work with people who are suddenly paralyzed from the neck or waist down, quadriplegic or paraplegic. These people experience their loss with a similar shock and pain that others feel in response to a loved one's death. But the awful time comes not so much when they finally believe they are paralyzed, as when they finally begin to suspect that the paralysis may be permanent.

In the same way, a person can believe he has cancer, he can know it is a fact of his life, but the deeper, soul-wrenching pain comes when he begins to suspect that the cancer is, without question, going to kill him. And so it is in the mourning process.

The person who has suffered great pain, finally believing in the death as a fact, now must face the truth that the death is permanent. We are very quick, in the literature, to point out that the small child cannot relate to the permanence of death. She can believe that the person she loves is dead, but the child still thinks that person will come "up again from the ground with the spring flowers." On the whole, we adults are not much different. Intellectually we know that death is permanent, but it takes us a long time to believe that death is permanent. And when this happens, like slow, choking fingers, "forevermore" gets hold of the mourner's mind and she doesn't know what to do with herself.

She has been a good mourner. She has talked it out. She has let friends listen to her, hug her, be with her, and do for her. She has had a wake and a funeral and acknowledged sympathy tributes. She has ordered a gravestone and visited the grave, or sprinkled the ashes and visited the site. She has suffered intense pain. She has done her part. Now why don't things get back to normal?

But normal, as normal was, is no more. The old equilibrium will never return. And slowly she begins to suspect that the reason it will not return is that the person she loves will not return. "Nevermore" is not just a word, it is a reality to be lived through. This brings her up so short that she stops her world in a different way; she enters the world of nothingness.

This is not a world with death or the dead person as an all-consuming, acutely painful focus. Neither is it a world with anything else as an all-consuming pain-releasing focus. It is a world filled with nothing.

The mourner now functions again in this world. She uses the tools of the world in everyday life. *But she does not experience the world*. She experiences only a deep, hollow ache and an intense inner wrestling with the phantoms of meaninglessness. Where once she was filled with pain, now she has been hollowed out. She is empty, and can find nothing but unanswered questions, half-senseless thoughts and profound doubts to put into that emptiness.

Most people make the mistake of thinking that when this time of hollow ache comes the worst is over for their friend. But it isn't.

This aching period of hurt can last a long time. And it is difficult to try to be a friend to someone in this phase of mourning.

Your friend will often withdraw into her own world, rarely reaching out or allowing you entry. If she does, however, you should give her as much listening time and encouragement to talk out her thoughts and feelings as you can.

Though your friend in mourning will still need you, she may also rebuff you at times, or seem to deal with you in a perfunctory or even inexplicably harsh manner. Attention to the amenities of politeness is simply too difficult to sustain for any length of time. She may tell herself that a month or two has passed and she should be getting back to normal, so at times, she may try. But if she feels she is still not functioning "correctly" she will become uncomfortable and want out, want to retreat, or to run away. And you may be left in mid-air.

To you it may seem as though she doesn't want your friendship any more. You may well wonder what you did to offend her. Nothing. Rest assured, you did nothing. Just hang in there and be patient.

Anne Brooks wrote during such a period: "I don't like anything. Not food, not friends, not music . . . I find faults in all my friends. Why did I ever like them?"[4]

The other thing your friend in the hollow ache of mourning may do, consciously or unconsciously, is compare all the people she knows with the person who died. And for now, usually *nothing* can compare. That person and that relationship have become nearly perfect. Nothing can take their place. This is difficult for friends who are trying to help; but it is normal.

The mourner's loss has become larger with the realization of permanency. And as the feeling of loss increases, so the dimensions of the dead person grow to fill that huge void. The dead person becomes nearly perfect in the mind of the mourner. The memories get better and better, happier and happier. You, as a merely mortal friend, may look puny by comparison with the now nearly canonized dead person.

Such feelings may be even more intense if a mourner is still feeling a secret guilt that she didn't love the dead person as much as her friends and family thought she did. So, she magnifies the perfections of the person and the relationship to compensate.

You may find that you hardly recognize the deceased in the words of the mourner; he may have taken on saintlike qualities. The relationship he had with the mourner may be depicted as far more blissful than you had ever perceived it to be. But for now, just listen and be glad that the lines of communication remain open. It may be possible at this time for other family members to introduce a more "well-rounded" picture of the deceased. But for you as a friend to do so now would be unwise.

Your friend's days and nights will seem to drag, especially her nights. Each morning, as she wakes, she will again be reminded of her loss. She may have dreamed of her dead loved one, especially if it was a spouse. Or she may even have had halluncinations of the dead person being present. Dreams and even hallucinations are normal and can be therapeutic in the mourning process, so long as the distancing from reality is not too extreme and doesn't last indefinitely.

Your friend may laugh, but rarely; and if she does she may feel guilty that she has done so, that she has appeared to experience a moment of pleasure. Her laughter will seem to her, in a strange way, a betrayal of the person who has died and the magnitude of his loss.

If you do hear your friend in mourning laughing, please don't look at her as though she has committed a sacrilege; don't even look surprised. Simply smile and say, "It's good to see you laugh. John would have liked that; he always liked so much to see you happy." This can make Mary feel that it is all right to laugh occasionally, and that John would approve.

A side-note on laughter in relation to tragedy or other sober events. I have a wild and wonderful stepdaughter who laughs when she is very nervous, embarrassed, uptight, or frightened. This is not something she has any control over. Biting her lip helps, but not always. There are others in the world like Nicole. If you see a mourner laughing during a funeral or wake, be sensitive enough to know that he is not doing this out of disrespect. He may be doing it because he cannot help it. At some level, it is a way to avoid crying, for the two are closely related emotionally.

Laughter can be very therapeutic, too. It can be a tremendous release of tension for everyone involved, especially at the wake or after-funeral gathering of a person who had long been known to be dying. The pressure in such cases has been building, and when death finally comes, laughter can provide much-needed relief, just as a flood of tears can be a release from shock numbness.

Though there may be occasional laughter, your friend in the ache of mourning is finding little or nothing about which to be happy. She is existing in the past, functioning in the present, and feeling that there is no future worth speaking of or looking forward to. Or, if she is thinking of a future, she may be re-evaluating her values and priorities in life. This is usually good; but done too obsessively and quickly, without proper perspective, it can lead to precipitous, unwise changes.

Also, many of the guilts, angers, and fears of the painful period of mourning are returning to haunt her, and these feelings are demanding to be dealt with at a deep level. *This is good, it must happen.* But the constant struggle to sort out and reevaluate those feelings as well as many of her values and priorities of life, leaves the mourner physically tired and emotionally drained.

Time and time you may notice that your friend will heave heavy sighs, sighs that really ask from some ache deep inside, "What am I doing and where am I going and who am I now and what does it matter anyway?"

The person may talk a lot of this out with God, either as God or as that power-somewhere-that-is-greater-than-any-one-person-event-or-thing. To the mourner this God may seem very far away at times and very close at others, so close in fact that were He any closer He might get a good punch in the teeth. And that's all right, God can take it, as the saying goes.

Another thing your friend in mourning is trying to do during this time of hollow ache is to unlearn her expectations about the presence of the person who died. Therefore, she needs to be alone at times to teach herself that she is alone, to confirm her awareness that something is permanently missing.

When someone close to us dies there are daily activities that are permanently altered by the absence of the loved one. And so we must unlearn old habits.

When I returned to work after Chris died, I didn't know what to do with myself when the end of the working day came. I wanted to be able to go into Chris's office and unwind and talk and laugh as we had done so often before. But Chris wasn't in his office. I assume I simply went straight home after work, but for the most part those times are blank in my memory. I blocked out that time of day for months until I could establish other patterns of living, other habits.

Friday nights were especially dreadful for me for a long time. I couldn't forget that Chris equaled Friday night until I was finally comfortable filling those evenings in other ways. I felt physically and mentally lost for many Friday nights.

Well-meaning friends tried to fix me up with new dates. I'm glad they did this, but I had to say no for a long time. Fortunately, they didn't give up. But it took me about a year before I could date with any interest again.

I do have recall of friends trying to help during this extended period of ache, and the recall is positive. But I know, too, how many times I rebuffed—politely, I hope—their attempts to help. It wasn't that I was up again, down again, though I'm sure that's how it appeared to my friends; I was simply nowhere stable.

At times I would go through the motions of doing something because it was easier than saying no, or because I thought it would help. But I didn't do anything because I wanted to. I didn't want anything. Now that I believed that Chris's death was permanent, I felt that if I couldn't have him I didn't want anything else. After all, he and our relationship had been nearly perfect.

But it is not easy to live for a long time in limbo; and it is not easy to live daily with perfection. That is why we put up monuments to our heroes and then go about our imperfect lives. But we do have to put up those monuments; and so, too, does the mourner come to feel that he has to *do something* to make the dead person's life still count. The mourner has to do something to make sure the dead person is not forgotten before he can be comfortable moving on.

But, before we discuss the doing phase, let's see what you can do to help your friend in mourning through the ache of hollowness, the ache of nothingness.

Your friend is probably aware of the feelings of hollowness and meaninglessness she is experiencing as she wrestles with her internal demons. You can help her simply by reassuring her that they are normal. You can be patient, and keep the doors of communication open. One time your friend may respond, the next she may treat you almost as if you were an unwelcome door-to-door salesman.

If she does respond, she may want to talk about any number of things. She may bring up happy memories of the dead person, and you can feel comfortable here and there to add to or reinforce these memories without trying to outdo your friend. She may want to rediscuss her guilts, angers, or fears. Listen first, then help her, if she asks, to reason through them as best you can. Even if you have discussed these with her before, don't remind her of that fact. She may not remember, or she may need to talk them through again at a deeper level.

She may want to discuss her questioning of life, of values, or of God in light of the death. This is normal and usually therapeutic. Caution your friend against making any major changes in her life in the first year; but otherwise just listen without being judgmental. And if you feel comfortable in this kind of discussion, let her know that questioning of or anger at God in this context is normal and understandable, even by God. Don't try to impose your religious beliefs on her, however, unless you are very sure she is asking for them. And even so, don't assume she will hear or adopt them. And don't be disapproving if she seems to lose faith for some time, and in some few cases, forever.

You can best be her friend by listening, being available, and not being judgmental.

One thing your friend will rarely discuss, however, if she responds to your open door of communication at all, is you. She doesn't mean to be self-oriented, but she is. For her the world stopped the day of the death, and though she is using its tools to live day by day, she had not really returned to being part of it. Her pain is her world, nothing outside exists.

This can be difficult for a friend who may well have her own needs, thoughts, and experiences, and want to share them. But if you can stay with it you'll be helping your friend in greater measure than you know.

If you try to communicate with your friend and are rebuffed, don't act insulted or angry, just leave gracefully and promise to come back again at a better time. In the interim you can send a "thinking-of-you" note. It doesn't matter whether it's a greeting card or a note in your own words. What matters is keeping the doors of communication open. The mourner now has a reason to call you if she's so inclined. If you don't hear from her it may be because she still doesn't want to talk, or because reaching out is simply too difficult or takes too much energy.

Call again after sending the card, perhaps a week or two later. Don't say, "Did you get my card?" as if a response was expected. Simply say, "I just wanted to say hi." You will, again, be able to tell from the person's response if she wants to talk.

Often friends, being afraid of saying or doing the wrong thing or calling at the wrong time, simply don't make contact at all. They may tell the mourner to call them if she needs anything or wants to talk. But rarely does the person in the hollow ache of mourning respond to this. Taking the initiative is just too difficult. Consequently, she can go for very long periods without any contact with her friends, and this contact can become more difficult to renew when the mourner is finally ready.

There is example upon example of mourners discussing how they had to bear the burden of reinstituting friendships with people who had stopped contact because they "didn't know what to say."

There is no absolutely right thing to say. "I've been thinking of you and I called to say hi. Is this a good day?" opens many a door as soon as there is any chance at all that the mourner could have a better-than-rotten day.

If you do have a fear of disturbing your friend in mourning by calling her, drop her a note saying in your own words something like, "I know things are still hard for you and I don't want to bother you when you'd rather be alone or with your family. But I'll call you occasionally just to say hi, and to let you know that I'm here if you want to talk or see me.

"But each time I call I'm going to ask if you feel like talking or not. Please tell me the truth. I promise you I won't be hurt or offended if you say you don't want to talk. I'll understand, and I'll still be your friend."

What you've done is given your friend freedom not to talk without jeopardizing the friendship. And when she does begin to heal, yours will be one relationship that she won't have to work to reinstitute. Actually, asking your friend if she wants to or feels like talking is a good rule of thumb when you initiate contact *at any time* during the mourning or dying process.

Another thing you can begin to do during this period of hollow ache is to give your friend opportunities to emerge and re-enter the social realm of life. Your first as well as fifth try will probably be refused; but don't give up. Don't push, but don't give up.

Consider what it was that you and she enjoyed in the past, especially if there was something that didn't involve the person who died. Perhaps you liked to bowl or go to movies together. Invite your friend to do this. If you bowled on a team, this may be too much for her. Simply suggest that the two of you go alone, to keep the situation and environment as uncomplicated and unpressured as possible. If it is a movie, choose the movie carefully, nothing too morbid or raucous. Don't add too many extras, like dinner before or drinks after. If your friend accepts, you may want to suggest one of these additions the next time.

The exact time your friend's loved one died, or times at which she regularly did something with the person who died, may be very difficult for her. You may want to occasionally call or stop by, or offer an invitation for these times, as long as you aren't trying to duplicate the same event they shared. The important thing, especially in this situation, is to give the person immediate permission to refuse your call, visit, or invitation. You may be surprised, however, at how open she may be to filling these hard times.

Resuming an activity the mourner shared with the person who died is usually the most difficult thing for her to do. Like laughing, it can give her the feeling of dishonoring the memory of the person who died, or even of cheating on him. This is irrational, but also very normal.

Finally, in time, the person in mourning will have re-entered daily life actively enough that she can resume doing with others things she had done with her loved one. But this may take a very long time. It can be a year or more in many cases, and in a few instances there are things a person will simply never do again. If she has otherwise returned to participation in daily living, her decision must be honored.

In summary, you can help a person through the period of hollow ache by acknowledging what she is going through and understanding that it is normal. You can keep doors of communication open and, with ongoing consistency, reach through them to your friend by telephone, in person, and/or through the mail. But you must always give her permission to say no to your call or visit without feeling that she is risking your friendship. If she chooses to talk, listen regardless of how often she may repeat herself. And help her reason through her guilt or other painful feelings again if she needs you to.

If your friend chooses to talk about basic life issues, listen without being judgmental. And if she's angry with God, and if you are comfortable doing so, let her know that that can be a normal reaction to feelings of human helplessness in the face of death, understandable even by God.

Also, you should be thick-skinned, knowing that one day your friend may respond to your communication and the next day she may not; and that rarely, if ever, will she respond to you as a person with feelings in your own right.

In time you can give your friend unpressured opportunities of short duration to re-enter active daily life, understanding that many of your offers will be refused.

Above all, be patient with your friend. She does need you. Soon again she will need all of you and you can begin to rebuild a sharing relationship.

But before a new equilibrium can be attained, while she is still aching, the person in mourning feels compelled to do something to assure herself that the person who died will not be forgotten.

What often brings about this compulsion is that for moments here and there the mourner, even in the midst of her deep, hollow ache, has drifted away from her suffering to thoughts completely unconnected with the loved one.

This has frightened her. Deep inside she begins to worry that she will forget the person who died, will forget the immensity of her loss.

Deep inside she wants to be relieved of her hollow ache. But she desperately *does not* want to forget the person whose death caused that ache. And odd as it may seem, she does not want to let go of the intensity of her feelings; however painful, they make everything else look insignificant. A close brush with mortality is terrifying—but it puts you in touch with the depths of your being, and after that it's hard to want to live on the surface again. It's not surprising that your friend experiences a tug-of-war between her obsession with the dead person and death—and a need to get on with life. One way of breaking this impasse is to do something to ensure that the dead person is not forgotten, something to make him live on—in memory—in the future.

The mourner will probably tell herself that she does what she does so that other people, society, or the world will not forget the person she loves, or so that others will benefit from the death of that person. But though that may truly happen, the real and perhaps subconscious reason she is doing something is to give herself an acceptable route out of the ache of mourning. By doing something that will ensure the dead person's permanence in the mourner's life, the mourner frees herself to return to active daily living.

This "doing something" is not always costly. But somehow it is aimed at reminding the mourner that the person she loved lived and left a lasting impression on her life and the lives of others.

When Chris died I did, or tried to do, several things. In the beginning these were personal things, personal tributes. Praying him through purgatory, as he had asked me to do, was my first attempt to do something, even though I was in shock denial and couldn't believe I was doing it any more than I could believe or comprehend the fact that Chris was dead.

For many mourners, fulfilling the request of a deceased loved one is a "clear mandate." It offers an avenue for doing something that was known to be desired by the deceased. At times, however, such requests are impossible or impractical to fulfill. It is better never to agree to a request involving after-death actions if that request appears improbable to fulfill. It can leave the mourner with an added sense of guilt rather than a tangible deed accomplished in tribute to the dead loved one.

Another effort to do something to honor Chris was my grave-sitting, part of my crazies. It evolved from my need to stop my world and be with Chris, but it was a literal acting out of my emotional struggle to give Chris back the qualities of a living person—feeling, hearing, seeing, and knowing.

When the intense pain passed on with the intense crazies and I not only knew Chris was dead, but knew that the loss was permanent, I still found it difficult to give him up. At least his memory had to stay alive in my mind. And I wasn't ready to forget the intensity of feeling I had experienced in my life as a result of Chris's death. That was another route to calling up his presence. Therefore, I felt I needed to do something to make sure I wouldn't forget.

As I sat in my office and thought of Chris, with this need to do something that said he wasn't forgotten, I decided to have a mass said for him for each date we had had for the entire year preceding his death. Week by week, month by month, I reviewed the year on my calendar, the same calendar from which I had torn the corner for my kiss.

Chris and I had dated a lot more than I had realized. Saying all those masses wasn't easy on my income! I had to pay by the month, but I did it. Telephoning to have masses said, donated anonymously, was doing something to keep Chris's memory alive. Knowing that the masses were being said on the anniversary of our dates was letting him—and me—know that he was not forgotten.

The other thing I did to keep Chris's memory alive was to visit his church each Sunday afternoon after his death for nearly two months. This wasn't easy. The church was a good distance from my apartment and I couldn't ask to borrow Jennifer's car every week. So I took the bus, buying an all-day transfer.

I would go in, hoping the church would be empty of anyone I knew, and sit where Chris and I had sat the one time we went to church together, not too long before he died.

(He hadn't thought I would go with him that time, and was pleased when I didn't hesitate. But I teased him royally because he had been going to church so often that month to earn indulgences. Here I'm sure Elisabeth Kubler-Ross would say that somehow Chris knew he was going to die soon. Perhaps she would be right; perhaps he did.)

I would sit in "our" pew those Sunday afternoons after Chris's death and pray some. But I would also just sit and be. Then I would light a candle for him and take the bus home. I saved every transfer in a small drawer in my desk. They are still there, but now they're part of my "history."

When the thought of going to Chris's church on Sunday afternoons first came to me it was natural, as if I was drawn there. It was such a normal thing to do, as was sitting by Chris's grave. Acting out a memory to preserve a memory. It was what I wanted to do.

But slowly, visiting Chris's church every Sunday afternoon began to seem like a duty. I began to notice how long the bus trip took. Once there, I found I sat for less time in the pew and I was more distracted by movement about me. But I wasn't able or willing to stop without putting something in the place of my churchgoing, without something else to assure that Chris would know, or I would know, that I had not forgotten him. I still needed to do something more.

In my mind, the idea was a natural one, and it certainly was a big one, equaled in scale only by my naïveté in thinking there was a snowball's chance in Florida that I would succeed.

Chris was a businessman who was also politically active in his community, though not in the "ruling" party of the city. In the neighborhood where he lived a school had recently been built. Chris had loved his neighborhood and was proud of the number of personal contributions he had made to improving it.

Therefore, since Chris was known in the community as well as in the political circles of the city, it seemed only logical to me that the new, as yet unnamed school should be named for Chris. That certainly would assure that he would not be forgotten, especially in the neighborhood he loved.

One of our favorite restaurants was one where a number of politicians ate. Invariably when Chris and I went there, someone in politics would come over and say hello to Chris. One man in particular, a man who worked high up in the ruling party in the city, often stopped to say hello and talk with us. It was to this man I turned with my "logical" request to name the new school for Chris.

Since I mentioned Chris's name in requesting to meet with this man for coffee at a nearby restaurant, I suspect that his willing agreement may have included a slight expectation of intrigue. I look back on it with a chuckle, thinking more clearly in retrospect, that he may have thought I was going to give him some juicy tidbit of political corruption. The man probably deserves a medal for not breaking into laughter at the naïve request that came instead.

But he kindly sympathized with me over Chris's death and said he certainly would try; although he could hold out no guarantees—let alone much hope—since there was always "a matter of politics in these things."

Imagine, thinking that a new school in a city dominated for years by one political party would be named for someone identified in the service of the opposition? But for years afterwards I received a Christmas card from that nice man. He probably hasn't come across such naïveté since.

I tell this story as an example of the mourner's need, before she can feel free to try to resume actively living, to do something she feels will keep the dead person's memory alive.

A few weeks later, the man from city hall told me as gently as possible that the new school was to be named for a former congressman. But, he added, "We tried."

And that was enough. I had tried. I had done things to keep Chris alive in my own memory and had tried to extend that to a city. But everyone who dies is not John F. Kennedy.

The bottom line is, simply and sadly, that even with plaques and masses and monuments, you cannot keep someone alive. Nor can you hold on to the intensity of feeling you had in the process of his dying or your mourning. But we need to try long enough to make a statement to ourselves; to the person, if he can in any way know; and to God, if He's listening—that the one we love is respected beyond the grave, that he still has meaning for us.

That statement is our attempt to say all the things we didn't say, to do all the things we didn't do, and to be all the things we think we never were to the person who died.

Your friend may or may not tell you of the things she is doing to keep alive the memory of the person who died or to hold on to the intensity of feeling she experienced surrounding the death. I told no one I knew of the masses, or the church visits; and to the day I wrote this I told no one but the man from city hall about naming the school. But that is me; and every person is different. If your friend tells you what she is doing or trying to do, be supportive, but don't lavish your praise on her; and without detracting, don't embellish the already saintlike qualities she may be attributing to the person who has died. For the more you heap praise on your friend for all she is trying to do, the more difficult it will be for her to stop when her need to act dissipates. The more you add to any saintliness the dead person may have acquired in your friend's eyes, the more difficult it will be for your friend to begin to remember her relationship in perspective and to risk forming new relationships with ordinary humans.

Another important way you can help your friend during this period is by pointing out to her the values visible in her life as a result of her relationship with the dead person. Focusing on values that were either instilled or enhanced in the mourner by the dead person helps demonstrate to your friend the ways in which the dead person lives on in her.

This is different from telling the mourner she must adopt the qualities or lifestyle of the dead person. This can be too great a burden and is unfair. It can even be dangerous or tragic if your friend, either through her own needs or the unthinking encouragement of friends, feels obliged to memorialize her loved one by taking on that person's unfinished business or trying to follow in his footsteps. In a few circumstances this can turn out all right. But if it threatens, submerges, or negates the individuality of your friend, it could be a major mistake and cause her internal heartache in the long run.

On the other hand, discussing enduring qualities that are part of the legacy of the dead person—a genuine living legacy—can help your friend understand that the groundwork for immortality for her beloved exists within herself. For regardless of plaques, schools, books, or monuments, what we leave behind of ourselves is that which has grown between us and others we have loved. There are many gifts and century upon century of people who loved within each of us; gifts which we will add to and pass on through our children and through others we love.

HEALING

Quiety one morning, with no bells, no trumpets, no fanfare, and likely with no notice, a new equilibrium will begin to return to your friend. It will not be the same as before, and it will not yet include equilibrium with people or things outside. Nevertheless, it will be the beginning of an internal equilibrium . . . and thus the beginning of healing.

Active, daily, all-consuming mourning will be over. Mourning will make many return visits to your friend, often unannounced. Disbelief, tears, pain, ache, the need to do—all the family of active mourning—will come back; but each will now limit its visits. Your friend won't feel so engulfed. There is no timetable for when this easing off occurs. The aching sensation lingers longest, and returns most frequently.

They say that time heals all wounds. That is not true. Time alone will heal nothing if a person does not go through active mourning when someone she loves dies. But mourning itself takes time, and once that time has elapsed, a comforting distance from death will have been traveled, and the raw edges of suffering will begin to be rounded off.

In time, and through mourning, a person most often will realize that though the fact of death is painful and cannot be changed, she would rather have loved the person who died, rather have shared his life for even the too short time they had, than never to have known him at all. The mourner will take with her the qualities of life that resulted from the relationship, and she will add those qualities to her relationships with others along the way, without forgetting the person who was their source or their enrichment in her life.

This healing is a result of active mourning and time, and it begins with fleeting moments of returning equilibrium. Your friend becomes aware that inside she is increasingly better able to cope with the day's events and intrusions. She may be able to accomplish a difficult task, such as cleaning out the dead person's desk, that she had been unable to do before. She will be better able to take in and retain information not related to the person who died or to his death. Her occasional laughter is rarely guilt-producing. Nature reminds her that it is still there: hot, cold, rain, sun, trees, and plants are again noticed and perhaps even appreciated. An occasional television program is watched rather than merely looked at, though humorous references to death often are not funny to the mourner. She can read more than one or two paragraphs of a book or newspaper without her mind wandering, though perhaps she still pays more than passing notice to the obituaries.

These and other clues make your friend begin to trust that her inner equilibrium is returning. This trust does not return overnight. Every time a hurt, a pang of mourning returns for a visit, her trust wavers. She even has moments of thinking equilibrium will never return; and it takes a long time for her to trust in it enough to enable her to respond to anything outside herself.

But that door of communication you have kept ajar for your friend will now draw her across its threshold. She will not have to work to reestablish communication with you. You and she will not have to wade through apologies to each other about why you haven't been in touch. You will have kept the door ajar even at times when it appeared that the opening was ignored, and you will have given her permission to ignore it until she was ready to come to you.

Your job was not an easy one, and you deserve a star in your crown for working hard on an unconditional friendship. However, your star won't come from your friend, not at first anyway.

The first time your friend responds to an invitation from you to do something social she will probably be scared to death of her own reaction and quite unaware of your feelings. But you may be scared too. Even if you maintained a relationship during the mourning process, your mutual ease may degenerate considerably in the face of an outing in a social context. But despite how apprehensive either of you may be, remember that your friend is showing how much she trusts you simply by being with you in this context.

When you do offer your friend an opportunity to venture out, she may not be ready, so don't pressure her. And when she does eventually join you, do not expect her to pronounce the occasion a success, even if she manages to stay through the entire event.

Most things we do socially are at some level frivolous. That's all right under normal circumstances. We all need some light moments in this crazy world. But when a person has been through the intensity of active mourning and has reached into the depths of her soul and fought it out with pain, fear, guilt, anger, emptiness, God, or all of these—when she has wrestled as Jacob with the angel—then going on a social outing, to bowl, to dinner or lunch, may leave her feeling that her time was wasted in worthless chit-chat.

A person coming out of active mourning and into the ordinary, human world is often very judgmental of that world. And she may make a number of false starts before she rejoins it with even a slight sense of comfort or equilibrium.

Recall the stop-start motion with which I physically responded when I first saw Chris in his casket. This stop-start way is how one often enters the frightening world of active mourning, and it is often the same way that she re-enters the now frightening world of everyday living.

Your friend may fear that the activities of ordinary life will rob her of the intense togetherness she felt with the loved one during mourning. And, for the most part, it will.

It takes an immense amount of energy to hover daily at the core of life-and-death feelings. When we are there we feel strangely alive, because the pain is forcing our every nerve to feel, to respond. We are in a way vibrating through our nerve endings with the struggle to stay alive and fight the pain of death, to wrestle with the unanswerable questions of human existence. It is too much. It is overload. We cannot do it day in and day out forever, unless our minds retreat. An end must come. And when it does, we will in large measure lose that intensity of feeling. We don't forget we had those feelings, and we may even retain and later act on priorities or quality-of-life issues that were influenced by those feelings. But we cannot hold on to that level of intensity and survive.

There are many different circumstances of mourning, and many different circumstances of re-entry. You may be trying to help a couple mourning the death of a child; or a widow or widower. These can be difficult social situations, since at times they can involve more than a one-to-one relationship. You can help by offering an unpressured situation of re-entry based on your own past activities together and on your friend's mourning situation.

One of the most gentle approaches is to make the person feel wanted in your social circle, but give her the chance to pick the setting the first time out. You could say something like, "I really want to see you sometime soon if you feel at all ready to risk an outing. And to keep it as unpressured as possible I would like to do whatever you think would make you feel the least uncomfortable. Maybe dinner just with me (or us), or with a few others if you would like; or maybe just come by for coffee. Next Tuesday or Thursday are good. I can pick you up. You tell me what would be best for you. The point is, if you're at all ready, I'd really like to see you."

You need not say all of that as a monologue, of course, Take cues as you go or improvise your own message. The important things are to make your friend feel wanted, to think of ways to keep the situation as unpressured as possible, to give her a choice of setting and day, to perhaps offer transportation, and to give a back door out either before or during the occasion. This last can be done at the end of the conversation, as a postscript, "And, Mary, if it gets too difficult for you, I (or anyone here) would understand if you call it an early night or cancel at the last minute. You're the only one who can know how you feel." Which is true.

If the invitation is accepted and there are several days or more between the invitation and the occasion, a booster phone call can help. Often, after accepting the invitation, a person has second thoughts, especially the first time out. You can help bolster resolve if you call at mid-point to reassure her that she is wanted, and let her know that though you realize it is a big step for her you're glad she's able to at least work on trying it. This may give a needed boost, but it still leaves a crack in the door for her to back out. And it lets her know again that you know this event isn't going to be an easy thing for her.

When your friend does arrive, you can help by not acting as though everything is back to normal or as if nothing has happened. Everything is not back to normal, and something did happen. To speak to this fact early on acknowledges it as fact, and as important.

"Mary, I'm sure it wasn't easy for you to come tonight." This type of acknowledgment opens the door but does not force prolonged discussion of the tragedy. However, Mary's husband's death should definitely not be the main topic of conversation the entire evening.

The idea is that Mary has risked coming out in order to think and talk about some things other than John's death. It can help if you plan in advance, therefore, some other things she may want to discuss.

At times during the evening you can risk opening doors just a fraction here and there to things that could lead to mention of John, especially to Mary's happy memories of him. Your own happy memories of John may be painful for her to deal with, simply because any thought of John that she hasn't already rehearsed internally is something new to deal with. It is good and therapeutic that these memories be called up, but they may cause a tearful response. If the tears do come, Mary can handle them, she's been doing so for weeks, maybe months now.

Don't ask, "Are you all right?" (It never ceases to amaze me how we can see someone sobbing, for any reason, and ask if they are all right.) Say something like, "It's so hard isn't it, each time a new memory comes up." That may be all you need to say. She may talk it out some; or she may choose to move on to other topics; or she could decide to leave. Regardless, don't feel guilty. You didn't cause the tears. You made possible the memory, a good memory. The fact of John's death caused the tears related to it. Other memories will come, and most likely other tears. There is no way around this.

If your friend does leave early, let her know you are glad that she came, even for a few hours. Then telephone the next day to say how glad you were that she joined you. Don't apologize for bringing up the memory. Just say you know the evening was difficult, but you hope each time she ventures out it will become increasingly less difficult. Tell her, too, that you are glad to have her as a friend.

If the conversation turns to the death once again, one question you can ask is, "What things have helped the most?" This can give you and any others present clues to any further help that may be needed. Most of all, it can help your friend focus on the positive aspects of the painful process from which she is emerging. Don't be hurt if she doesn't specifically single out anything you did in her answer about things that were helpful. When we're in the forest we don't often remember to thank it for having trees. The fact that she made an outing with you is her thanks, her gesture of trust in you.

After your friend does venture out for the first time, doing something socially likely will never again be as difficult for her. That hurdle will be past, even if she does then retreat for a while. As a friend, just keep the door of communication ajar with an occasional phone call or note and eventually with another invitation.

There are some circumstances in mourning when a person will re-enter the social world without much hesitation. To some observers this easy re-entry may seem premature. If your friend chooses to re-enter social situations at a time earlier than you feel is "appropriate," you should nevertheless welcome her return and make her feel wanted and accepted. To measure an "appropriate" mourning response is dangerous and unfair.

One more comment before we leave social situations. I have a personal complaint on behalf of people who are widows, widowers, single or divorced . . . about how unfairly they can be treated socially. We seem to have come little distance from Noah's Ark in our continuing need to entertain by twos. Heaven forbid there be an odd number of people at the dinner table. Heaven forbid two men or two women have to sit side by side. (They may enjoy their conversation for a change!)

In our home we have an ironclad rule (which my husband now thinks was his idea) that no party we host will be based on couples for couples' sake. If someone does not have a partner and he or she is our friend, that person is invited either to come alone or bring a date of his or her *own* choosing.

Obviously, one wouldn't invite someone newly widowed to bring a date. A person widowed or divorced will let you know in time if they are "keeping company."

But not to invite a person at all to anything involving couples because he or she is not (or not now) part of a couple is ridiculous. A married person is not half a person and neither is a single or divorced or widowed person half a person. End of lecture.

Having begun to feel some equilibrium of living, both inside and outside, your friend will have one final thing to do: she will have to integrate what has happened to her into her life. She will have discovered that the equilibrium of living that is returning is not the old equilibrium. Things are not the same. The path of the life before her has changed. She will not do all the things she might have done had the person she loved not died, but she will do other things that she might never have done before the death. Equilibrium may be returning, the activities of daily living resumed, but all is changed, irrevocably.

As all this is happening, one day your friend will notice you once again—not just as a pair of ears or hands for her—but as you. She may thank you very clearly for all you have done—the star in your crown, as it were—or she may never realize how hard you worked to help her, but merely sense that she is comfortable being with you, doing things with you, or talking with you again. And that must be thanks enough for you.

She will not forget the person who died and you cannot hurt her by sharing memories or giving her opportunities to talk about that person, both now and in years to come. Open the door to the subject gently; she'll go though it if she chooses. If she does not, gently close it again. Don't be afraid to mention the dead person's name if it comes up naturally in the course of conversation. It would be more awkward to stop talking abruptly and change the subject. The name will have surfaced in both your minds by then regardless. The person did, after all, live.

You'll find yourself very glad when reintegration returns for your friend and equilibrium returns to your relationship. There hasn't been a lot in this whole process for you. It took a great deal of energy to be a friend to your friend these many months. But you did receive two benefits: You know you have it in you to be a friend when a friend is needed. And your friendship may be all the stronger in the long run for the work you put into it. If ever you find yourself in your friend's place, you may realize yet a third benefit—that she will be there for you, as you were for her.

4

Children in Mourning

WE CAN MAKE a major mistake when we assume that children express mourning the same way and have the same needs as do adults. Children, like adults, usually do experience shock, hurt, and healing during the process of mourning, but they often express them differently, and need a different kind of comforting.

A child of any age will be better able to understand death and deal with his own mourning if he has come in contact with death *before* someone close to him dies. But though we are willing and even eager to teach our children about many problems they may face in life, we usually have little or nothing to say to them about death until it happens to someone close to them. At this juncture we are usually in distress ourselves, and not always able to think clearly about how best to approach the tragedy with our children. We may make the mistake of telling them the bad news in their own room or other favorite spot, thus leaving them to associate a sad memory with that spot for perhaps many years. Then we may unintentionally ignore them for weeks to come because we are so swallowed up by our own grief.

Looking back, I realize how wise my mother was when she decided to take me to Mr. Keefer's funeral when I was only about six. She says she doesn't remember; but I can picture parts of that afternoon as if it were happening now.

* * *

I held my mother's hand as we went up the many steps to the church door. Mr. Keefer had died, and we were going to pay our respects to him.

I don't recall how my mother explained what dying was, other than I knew that Mr. Keefer wouldn't be in church any more because he had done it—he had died. He was old, and he had simply died, my mother said. It hadn't hurt him to die, and being dead didn't hurt him either, so I didn't have to worry about that.

Mr. Keefer had seemed very old to me, and I think he probably was. He used to say hello to me after church every week and often gave me a piece of chewing gum. I identified him with church and chewing gum. But now he wouldn't be at church any more except for today, and he wouldn't be able to give me any chewing gum today because he was dead.

My mother told me that Mr. Keefer would be lying down in a casket—I would see what that was—and that he wouldn't move and his eyes would be closed like he was sleeping, but he wasn't, he was dead.

I held my mother's hand even tighter and we went inside the vestibule of the old stone Lutheran church. I remember there was a shiny, black rubber runner on the wooden floor, and to the left of the door was the shiny, black casket with Mr. Keefer lying inside with his eyes closed.

But he didn't look to me like he was sleeping. He looked dead. Now I knew what dead looked like.

The child who sees a dead adult will never be confused and think that person is asleep. You can't fool a child. They see ten things for every one we see; they don't miss a thing. Children are very literal, very concrete. Seeing a dead adult, they will see what death looks like, they will know it is not sleeping.

Having seen a dead person and being told that dead people don't come back to life on earth, the child will accept that fact.

But my story of Mr. Keefer is not over. We stood back from the casket for a few moments. I didn't say a word, and still held tightly to my mother's hand. Then my mother gently moved, as if to go closer. I didn't pull back, so we went. If I was thinking anything during this time, I can't remember. But I doubt if I was; seeing was enough.

. Then my mother asked me if I wanted to touch Mr. Keefer. "You don't have to be afraid, it's just nice, old Mr. Keefer, he wouldn't hurt you. Just pat his hand good-bye if you want.'' I did. And then I think we left, though I don't remember for sure.

It may be that my mother thought a viewing was enough, a mini-viewing before the service in the church. Or maybe we did go to the service and I don't remember it. I only remember, vividly, seeing and touching Mr. Keefer in his shiny, black casket in the church vestibule with the black rubber runner, and holding my mother's hand throughout.

In a few minutes I had seen what death looked like and it hadn't frightened me. I wasn't frightened because, for one reason, I didn't love Mr. Keefer. I liked him, but he belonged to one or two minutes of a Sunday morning, not to my day-in-day-out living. Also, my mother explained what to expect, how Mr. Keefer would look, beforehand. And, my mother held my hand throughout, offering me a feeling of security. She also did not force me to look, move forward, or touch. And finally, she let me know death—Mr. Keefer—wouldn't hurt me.

Little children can think of death as a boogy man; they can think it's like going to sleep; they can think it hurts; they can think it's catching; they can think it's not permanent; and they can think that they caused it to happen. These and many other misconceptions and fears of death can go through the young child's mind, and often none are dealt with until a death comes into his own family, the very time when adults' resources are stretched thin.

My mother, in her wisdom, exposed me to death before I had to mourn it. She did so with someone I had known and liked, so that I could see the difference between Mr. Keefer dead and Mr. Keefer alive, and could experience some loss, but not very much. She exposed me to the death of a person, which helped me know that people, like birds, animals, and insects, die. She also let me know that death in and of itself didn't hurt, and that it wouldn't hurt me to touch a person who was dead. She explained that death wasn't like sleeping—something I knew when I saw. And, therefore, I never worried that when I or my parents went to sleep we would die. She told me that death was permanent, and seeing helped me to accept that.

Giving a young child a minimally threatening experience of death, that of either a person or an animal; being with him for security; and answering any questions he may have can later prove to be a great help to him in facing the reality of death if someone he loves should die.

One other thing which may not surface, or which may seem to be problematic in giving a child a supportive, non-threatening death experience is explaining the cause of death, and the separation of body and soul (if that is the family's belief system). While mother didn't explain exactly what caused Mr. Keefer's death, I guess I assumed it was what happens when one gets very old; which is all right. Nor did she then try to explain the body and the soul and heaven. She just said that it was the last time Mr. Keefer would be in church and then he would go to live with God.

At six, that was enough. You don't have to over-explain; just give concrete, simple facts. If, at that age, I had wanted to know more I would have asked. But anything more offered in the way of explanation would only have confused me and taken away from the basic fact of death my mother wanted me to experience in a concrete way, without having to mourn greatly.

For some children, though, explaining the cause of death may be important. The child may have had bad thoughts about the person who died, or even have wished the person dead. Children do this, even with their parents. If that person then dies, the child may believe he caused the death. *It is important to let children know that you can't cause someone to die by wishing him dead or thinking bad thoughts about him.*

To help prove this, if there is any question, you can play a game with the child. Ask him to think very hard that you will sing, laugh, or cry. He will think, and you will not follow him. Ask him to tell you, "I wish you would sing" several times, even to the point of anger. You do not sing. Thus you will have explained to the child that he can't cause someone to do something merely by thinking or saying it, even with anger. So it is with dying: wishing it or saying it cannot cause it to happen.

The younger the child, the more difficult it is for an adult outside her immediate family to be her friend in any direct sense during mourning. A young child cannot comprehend how we can love many people. She loves her mommy and daddy, sisters and brothers, and grandparents. For a young child, under six or seven, to say of her own volition to an adult other than her parent or grandparent "I love you" is somewhat unusual.

With this in mind, let's look at some of the mourning responses and needs of children to see how a friend might help.

I was single for a number of years—thirty-six—before I married. With the marriage came one husband and two teenage stepchildren. Over the years, though they brought trials and tribulations, my stepchildren and I have become very close. I can say that I genuinely love them and that they appear to feel the same toward me, at least most of the time! But there is no question, nor would we want there to be, that they love their own mother in a unique and far deeper way.

The simple point is that no matter what her age or family situation, a child loves in a unique way those persons whom she defines as mommy and daddy.

The *very young* child can, however, in circumstances involving the death of a parent, identify more than one person as mommy or daddy in her lifetime. If, for example, a child is between eighteen months and two years of age and the person she has always known as mommy has died, there is a chance that if her father remarries within one to two years, she can grow to identify the second woman as her mother also. This does not negate the child's unique relationship with her real mother. She will remember her, usually through photos and stories, with feelings a child would have for a mother. But the living object of her mother/child love will now be the second mother.

This is because, to put it as simply as possible, the *very young* child identifies as the object of her love the person who regularly and predictably meets her basic needs. Usually this is the mother at first and then both parents. The very young child gets her initial identity from this early relationship. She is a part, in a literal sense, of her permanent care-givers because she is totally dependent upon those persons for her survival and nurturing.

As she gets older and increasingly is able to meet her own basic needs, she becomes aware of herself as an entity separate from her care-givers. But she still draws nurturing, reality testing, elements of personhood, and help with the daily complexities of life from her parents (or primary care-givers) for a number of years, well into her teens.

The person in her late teens, who is chafing to get out on her own, is a far different person from the eighteen- to twenty-four-month-old who is happily sure that mommy and daddy can meet all the needs in her life.

What does all this mean when a child's parent has died and you are trying to be a friend? I hesitate to suggest by age categories, since children mature on different timetables. But the child six or under, in most instances, will need to be given permission to mourn and be helped to verbalize and act through that mourning *by her remaining parent*. And the most effective way of being her friend is by being a friend to that parent. This is the ideal situation, though obviously it cannot and does not happen in every case.

If, as sometimes happens, a child is young and there is no one in the family who can be a consistent primary care-giver, during the post-death frenzy—feeding, dressing, bathing, and playing with her—you could offer to do this, if you are able.

Eventually a permanent, primary care-giver will have to be found. But in the busy time immediately surrounding a parent's death, all of these things can fall to whomever happens to be handy. And this can be very frightening to a child, especially if the person who has died has been her primary care-giver. In those circumstances it is particularly important that a child's sense of loss and fear be alleviated by having one person to rely on instead of a great number of people trying to meet her needs in haphazard fashion, which can be overwhelming. Keep in mind that children as young as six months will have identified their primary care-giver, and can suffer feelings of loss if that person disappears.

Ideally, primary care is immediately assumed or continued by the surviving parent. The next best solution is to turn over responsibility to a person whom the child already knows, such as a housekeeper, regular baby-sitter, or *sometimes* an older sibling. If you are a regular baby-sitter for a very young child whose parent has died, or have spent a lot of time one-on-one with the child, know that you can be immensely helpful by offering to care for the child as much as possible until the family can make other, more permanent arrangements.

But to my knowledge, beyond this special circumstance, the best way you can be a friend to a young child whose parent has died is by being a friend through the remaining parent and/or the person providing primary care.

This help can often be given by doing. The surviving parent is in mourning also, and he may not even be aware of his young child's feelings of loss, longing, and bewilderment. (Many adults think children six or under are too young to mourn. But this is not the case. It has been proven in many studies, including the classic *A Child's Parent Dies: Studies in Childhood Bereavement* by Erna Furman.[5] This is an *excellent* work, but somewhat difficult for a laymen to wade through.) Your help in doing, such as cooking, laundry, shopping, etc., can free the surviving parent to be with his child. That parent, possibly in numb shock or pain, is usually open to having things done for him.

You could say something like, ''I have a feeling you've been trying to get some quiet time to talk with Billy; he looks like he could use his daddy. Why don't I clean up here and you can go off somewhere with him and close the door. I'll make sure you're left alone for a while.''

This can do several things. Practically speaking, it makes it easier for the parent to take time to be with his child. Also, it can literally remind the parent that his child is there and needs him. The child will benefit from the attention, and the parent may benefit from being needed, for often he may be feeling helpless and useless and impotent in the face of death. Being able to do something for someone else can restore at least a small feeling of control.

For you as a well-meaning friend to go off to a quiet room with the young child is a second or even tenth best. That child needs most to be with someone he loves, because it is usually only from such a person that he will take permission to mourn.

In summary, in trying to be a friend to a child in mourning who is six years or under, the best way you can help is by doing things that will give his remaining parent or primary care-giver more time to spend with him.

In trying to be a friend to a child in mourning who is over six years old, the first question to ask is what is *your* age, and then what is your relationship to the *child*, not only to his parents.

Why does age matter? At times and with certain relationships it doesn't. But during some periods of adolescence a child simply does not feel comfortable talking to anyone more than ten or fifteen years older than him. In trying to deal with his fast-expanding world—his approaching adulthood and its responsibilities—and with thousands of unknowns suddenly staring him in the face, the adolescent can try to control that world by narrowing the range and types of people he will trust with his thoughts and feelings.

Adolescence is probably the most vulnerable time of life, and if you are over thirty, there is a good chance that someone thirteen or fourteen, or even sixteen or seventeen won't of his own volition talk to you about how he feels. Favorite teachers and much-loved housekeepers are occasional exceptions to this rule.

If you feel you may have a close enough relationships with a child over six to enable him to trust you with a part of his mourning, it is important for you to make early direct contact with that child.

Most people send sympathy cards or flowers to the so-called primary mourner "and family." There are times when this is all right. But if a child's parent dies he may well be feeling his loss as deeply as—or more than—the surviving parent. If you feel especially close to a child whose parent has died, send one sympathy card directly to the child and another to the remaining parent. You may follow this very soon or much later, depending on the relationship, with a low-key, brief telephone call directly to the child. If that goes well, you could offer an invitation to take a walk or get some ice cream. (Nutritionists notwithstanding, children often associate ice cream with soothing.) Don't ask an adult to inquire if the child wants to go. Ask him directly; otherwise he may feel forced or be forced to go, which can make him feel manipulated. (Be sure he has permission to go with you, however; and that those responsible know where he is going.)

If the child goes with you, don't start talking right away about the death of the parent. In fact, you don't have to talk much at all; just walk with him for a while. Don't touch him unless he initiates the action. Many children aren't used to and don't like to be touched by anyone other than parents or other family members. If you feel compelled to say something, ask, "Want to talk?" or "This sure is a rough time, isn't it?" He usually will say only yes or no, and may go no further without prompting.

Teenagers, especially, tend to talk to adults in sentences of one syllable. But that's all right. The fact that the teen has agreed to be with you, especially if you're over thirty, is monumental. Maybe you could go to an ice cream place where they have computer games. Play a few games with him if he wants. This can help him release energy. Or, you could toss a football around. If he talks about his feelings at all, mostly listen; and perhaps help him find or feel comfortable using certain key words, such as "angry" or "guilty" or "scared." At times children need help and permission to use the "heavy" words that truly describe their feelings. But *don't push* him to use these words or express such feelings. And don't jump in with a lot of advice of "I-remember-when's." If your parent did die when you were young, you can say so (without saying, "I know how you feel"). But stop there.

If he's curious to know how you felt or what happened when your parent died, he'll ask. But more probably the thought of you ever having been his age and having parents as young as his may be more than he can fathom.

If he doesn't talk about feelings, do not consider this time lost. You have said you care by taking time to be with him. By sending a sympathy note, you have made him feel that you know he suffered a loss. But you haven't embarrassed him in person or bugged him to talk about his parent's death when he didn't feel like it. You have helped.

Unless he opens up a great deal and seems to have a need to do more of this, the one outing is probably enough for a while. Moving slowly with children, especially if they are adolescents, is better than moving too quickly.

One area in which to exercise caution: You may have known the child's dead parent for years, had many more years of experience with that person than the child has. Some children, like most adults, will want to hear about your memories at some point; but other children may not, or may not wish to hear yet. So before you start talking about how you remember the dead parent, ask the child if he wants to hear.

Say something like, "I know you have some very special memories of your dad; he certainly was a fun man. I can remember some fun things he did, too, though I'm sure they're not as good as your memories. But if you ever want me to tell you, just ask." The child may not ask at the moment. But the offer has been made and she has been given the opportunity to ask later.

Be particularly careful of offering memories of the dead person to a younger child. Just as she may have been possessive of her parent in life, so she may cling to his memory in death, and not want to hear anyone else's memories, or to deal with the fact that someone else may have more memories.

Though the child may not want to think you have more memories of her daddy than she, she may on the other hand be happy to go to the zoo with you on Saturday just like she did with her daddy. For an adult mourner, it may be very difficult to resume activities or return to a favorite spot he shared with his dead love. But for a child this is often not the case. Doing so may help her keep memories of her father alive, and you are a vehicle—especially if you are male—to do this. Even some adolescents enjoy this kind of activity. But in any case never assume it is desired without asking.

Another way to help a child old enough to write is to give him a diary. Some children keep diaries regularly, others never. Either give or send the diary with a sympathy note saying something like, "I would guess you're having a lot of thoughts right now. Sometimes it helps to write them down and keep them in a drawer somewhere."

It is as important for a child to see his dead parent's body as it is for the adult to see the body of someone he loves. Even children as young as four or five can be given a choice as to whether to do this. *But what to expect must be explained to them thoroughly beforehand, and they must be given the freedom to change their minds or leave right away if they want*. Some known primary care-giver or remaining parent *must* be available to accompany the child and deal with his reactions.

The viewing of the body, especially for younger children, should be conducted apart from any ongoing wake. A child should be offered privacy. If a child wants to put a note or special trinket in the casket with the parent, there is no reason to discourage this. Children at any age should not be *forced* to view the dead parent's body. But especially for children over six, a viewing can be immensely helpful in dealing with the fact of death.

Some children do not have bad reactions to their parents' funerals. Younger ones may even feel a strange sense of importance. This is normal. Being a relative of the reason all these people have gathered, getting a lot of attention, and riding in a huge, black limousine with people opening doors for them may reinforce this feeling. The young child can get caught up in the newness of the funeral experience and put aside, for a time, the active awareness of its purpose.

Other children find the funeral to be an awful experience: A bunch of strange adults, many of them crying (even though it wasn't their parent who died); a minister they may not know describing their parent in ways they had never thought of, whispered conversations from which they are excluded. These children want to stop everything and run home and be with just their families.

(If only ministers performing funerals where children are present would say something directly to the children. It would help—maybe just a little—but it would help.)

So the viewing is over and the funeral is over and the child thinks that finally he can go home and be alone with his family, be as normal as possible again. And what happens? He finds the minister and the same group of people, some still crying, have all come along to his house.

They hug him and kiss him and tell him how sorry they are, and how he's such a brave little kid, and how he'll have to take care of his mommy, or sister, or somebody from now on, or any number of those other things we have said to children when we didn't know what else to say.

The after-funeral gathering can be of great comfort to an adult mourner. It can be an occasion to release tears and get shoulders or arms of support. It can be a time to talk out feelings or repeat and repeat and repeat. It can be an opportunity to be reminded, merely by the *number* of caring people present, how beloved was the person who died.

But for the child, in almost all cases, this gathering is the worst thing that could happen after the funeral. And the more people present, the worse it is.

There are several things a friend can do to help this situation, but some should be preplanned for better results. If there is any way the remaining parent and children can leave the burial grounds first and have some quiet time together at home, it should be arranged. People who arrive during that quiet time can be told that the parent and children need to be alone together for a little while, and that if they could stay in the front part of the house (or wherever), that will be appreciated. You as a friend could offer food and drink to the guests in the meantime.

It will help if the parent or primary care-giver can explain to the child that people will come to the house after the funeral out of respect for the dead parent and for the family. It should be explained that this is a custom and that it will be helpful to the remaining parent. But the child should be given permission to choose to remain in another part of the house for part or all of the gathering.

If the child chooses not to go, he should not be made to feel guilty. It can be explained that the parent will have to go but that he will return when the gathering is over and then they can have some more time together alone.

Children get hungry even when they are suffering. Food should be brought to those who choose not to join the gathering. This will make them feel included and remembered, and will replenish the energy that mourning takes from them.

Another way you could help is to arrange for a friend of the child's own age to spend time with him during the after-funeral gathering. The child in mourning could also be sent to his friend's home, and in some instances this may be better. But usually the child needs reassurance that the family won't disintegrate further, and he has a need to be at home.

If all else fails and you see the child at the after-funeral gathering being pummeled by well-meaners, or hiding in a corner, you could ask if he would like to take a walk, or show you his room, or do something else that he is interested in. This gives him the chance to get away and talk about something else, or not talk at all. If you do leave with the child, be sure the parent or someone with the parent knows.

Never make comments to the child such as, "Mommy's watching you from heaven" or "Daddy will know everything you do now." And don't tell the child he has to be a "Little Daddy" now and take care of Mommy or his sisters and brothers. These and similar comments are common and well-meaning, but can put way too much burden on the child, who may well take them literally.

Ideally children want to and should be able to do their mourning with the remaining parent, crying with that parent at times, and at other times crying by themselves, knowing from the parent that this is OK and acceptable. Others will mourn more with siblings, but not always.

Siblings may react very differently to mourning, depending on their age. A smaller child can crawl up on a parent's lap and get cuddled and hugged. An older child may desperately need to do that, but feel too big. So he'll weep more often as a vehicle to being hugged and cuddled by his parent.

One child may hide his sadness by showing intense anger;

another by acting out or withdrawing. You may be puzzled by such inappropriate responses, but remember that the child, like his elders, is entitled to his own form of the crazies. However, it is important that an adult help the child to uncover and deal with his sadness, or it could become buried and bring more severe problems later. (Children who act out, withdraw or are intensely angry for a long period of time should be given *professional help* to deal with their mourning.)

Some mourning children will be able to share their mourning with peers; but usually only one or two peers. Some children may mourn with an older child or young adult, say someone two to five years older, who seems like a wiser member of his own generation. Having such a person to turn to can make a child feel important (because someone so sophisticated is interested in him!), and can encourage him to discuss feelings he might not mention to anyone else.

Remember: Children do mourn—they feel shock and pain and healing—but they do so only at certain times and with certain people—and almost always only when permission to mourn has been given. However, the child does not have the same inner resources for dealing with tragedy that an adult does. Consequently the child mourns more sporadically, more slowly, in order not to be overwhelmed, and therefore *the child usually takes longer to complete his mourning process than the adult does*. We should not assume that because he is no longer talking about the death or the dead person the child is OK and has completed his mourning. This is especially true if he is showing any major signs of personality or behavior change, such as falling grades in school or acting out. Even if apparently unconnected with the death, such changes indicate that the child is still grappling with his grief.

In his peer group the child usually tries desperately to remain in tune. He may be the only one in the class to have lost a parent to death. Other children may stay away from him because in a strange way, they are afraid that he is catching; that if it could happen to his parent it can happen to theirs, too.

The last thing a child wants is to be set apart from his peers. Children spend a great amount of energy trying to be one of the group, and having a parent die can threaten this acceptance, and even cause irreparable damage.

Unless you are his teacher, you really can't help him much

with this other than to understand his feelings and try to treat him as normally as possible. As his teacher, you can help by asking the child how he would like to have the situation handled. You might offer to meet with those of his peers who know about the death. If he likes that idea, you can offer guidance by helping his peers talk out any misconceptions they may have of death, and helping them understand that Billy is still Billy and wants to be treated normally. Billy can attend such a meeting or not, as he chooses.

Children are great mimes. If a teacher can impress on two or three key children some facts about death, and encourage them to respond to Billy in a normal way, most of the rest of the class will follow suit.

The need for being treated normally comes not only in school, but at home too, where the child has a need to keep things as much as possible as they were. His world already has come unglued. It will only seem worse if the family now moves, or celebrates holidays differently, or fails to maintain any number of other family traditions, such as a week each summer at the lake or winter skiing trips.

This can be a nightmare for the remaining parent who sees things differently, who can hardly bear to think of doing things the same way without his spouse. Survival is best faced with compromise and with meeting the situation head-on by preplanning.

The rule of thumb mentioned earlier is not to make any drastic changes, such as a move or complete home redecoration, in the first year. If the parent can maintain this much stability, it will leave the child assured that all of his roots will not come up in a handful. But if the parent simply must make major changes, it is helpful to try to keep some remnants of old traditions.

As an example, suppose the family always went skiing over Christmas and celebrated the holiday in the mountains, always with hot chocolate and carol-singing. Perhaps the trip must be cancelled, but the hot chocolate and carols could stay.

Or, if the dead person's belongings must be disposed of, perhaps the child could be given a chance to choose two or three things of his parent's that he wants to keep as mementos. If there are very young children, it is nice if the remaining parent puts away some things for them to "grow into," like a fishing rod or special sweater. (As a friend, you may find the right moment to suggest this if you feel your friend may not have thought of it).

If you are a teenager reading this book, you have a great opportunity to help a friend who has lost a parent by treating him normally when you are together in a group. You can also give him some openings and rap-time when there's just the two of you. Talk about how he feels and what it was like to lose his parent, but without making him feel like he is a space cadet because of some of his feelings.

If you are a parent, please teach your child about death in some way that is nonthreatening. And teach your children not to tease, or ignore, or make any child experiencing mourning feel less a part of the group.

Just two more notes about children in mourning. Not every child likes to go to visit his parent's grave. To some it is an ugly, cold place, in no way connected with any happy memories they may cherish. Other children like to visit the grave. It may be where they talk to the parent or take flowers, or just feel a warm presence.

It is important to give a child opportunities to visit his parent's (or loved one's) grave. But he shouldn't be forced or made to feel guilty or bad if he chooses not to do so. On the other hand, adults who do not like to visit graveyards often forget to ask a child if he wants to go. As a friend, you could let the parent or care-giver know that you would be available to take the child at times if he cannot.

And finally, let's not forget anger. Anger at the dead parent is a big factor in a child's mourning. It must be acknowledged as normal and he must be given the freedom to express it. This is best done by the remaining parent; but at times that can be too difficult, especially if that parent is in the process of nearly sanctifying his partner as a part of his own mourning process.

This anger crosses all age groups, but may be more painful to deal with in children six and under. They are the ones in particular need of their widowed parent's permission to mourn. And that is the very parent who is indirectly also giving permission for justified anger to emerge.

The young child will feel abandoned by the parent who died, and this feeling of desertion will make him angry and lead him to direct his anger not only at the dead parent for dying and abandoning him, but for a litany of failures during his lifetime—such as not spending more time with him, not taking him to the movies as promised, and so on. He may also be angry with the remaining parent for changes in that parent resulting from the mourning process.

This anger is normal but can be very painful to the surviving parent, especially when he must give permission to the young child to express it. The remaining parent will need to explain that the dead parent did not choose to abandon the child; but he must also agree gently that, yes, it is too bad that you and mommy didn't have more time together.

If the parent's death was by suicide, this anger could be accompanied by a real and intense fear that the remaining parent will also commit suicide and, therefore, also abandon the child. A great deal of reassuring from the remaining parent is necessary here.

The surviving parent should not make promises that he will change overnight or do better at spending time with the child, because the child will remember this and the parent may not be able to do it. A child remembers positive promises longer than Methuselah lived.

Giving the young child a chance to vent his anger helps him through the mourning process. He will get over that anger much faster if he is given permission, especially by the remaining parent, to get it out, and general confirmation when aspects of it are reasonably justifiable.

The older child's anger mostly likely will not surface in as direct a manner. For some children, professional help is needed to get this and other feelings of mourning out. But anyone with a very close, trusting relationship to the older child, who, without judgment, can give him room to express his anger at his parent for dying and possibly at his remaining parent for mourning so much, can help greatly. The child should be helped to understand that his feelings of anger are normal and that he need not feel guilty about them.

If the parent's death was suicide, the older child may be even angrier—and guiltier. He may reproach the dead parent for not talking over his or her fears and/or unhappiness with the child and giving the child "a chance to help." The older child may also be fearful that his parent's suicide is in some way hereditary. This fear can linger into and through adulthood and pose real danger if it is not dealt with in a therapeutic setting. In general, it can be a very good idea to get professional counseling when the death is by suicide, for the feelings of both the remaining parent and the child will be especially intense and complex.

A few years ago, when my stepdaughter Nicole was not quite sixteen, I had to make a speech to two hundred teenagers about her same age. I was speaker at an ecumenical service to which those who didn't go to Mass were *forced* to come. In my entire speaking career I have never been faced with a greater nightmare! I agonized for weeks about what to say that would at least keep them awake and quiet. Then I realized an expert was living right under my nose.

I asked Nicole what, in her opinion, kids her age were most worried about. Her answer, a few moments later, stunned me: "The possible deaths of their parents." But I took her word, made that my main subject, and got two standing ovations.

Don't underestimate the depth of a child's mourning. But help him get it out in *his* way, which will be different from the adult's.

5

When a Husband
and Wife Are
Both in Mourning

SOME MEN CAN mourn actively in the ways described in the first part of this book. They move through the shock of denial and numbness, through physical pain and the pain of fear, anger, guilt, and tears. They ache for a long period, feeling at times that nothing will help and nothing is of lasting value.

Men, too, will try to do something to give permanent meaning and memory to the person's life. And they will reach new equilibrium and be able to incorporate the tragedy into their lives and move on. Other men may have more trouble mourning. For them, there may be an unusually large gap between the time they believe the death has occurred—when numb shock ends—and the time they are able to act on that belief—when they begin to feel and show hurt and start the process of active mourning.

And yet other men have such difficulty initiating or completing mourning that they need professional help.

Two major factors usually contribute to this overall problem. Many men by nature, tradition, or expectation feel inhibited about displaying or discussing feelings. Some men may even have *lost the ability to feel* because they were forced to suppress their feelings for so many years. And often men have, or feel that they have, the primary responsibility for leading and providing for their families. They feel pressured to bear all burdens.

Modern society is moving in a direction which offers men more freedom to discuss and display feelings without appearing weak or unmasculine. But in practice, men are often still put in the role of the strong leader, the decision-maker, and the provider, who must remain in control at all times.

If someone dies who is loved equally by both a man and a woman—the logical example here is a child—both parents will initially be in the shock of denial, then numbness. Both will at some point come to believe the fact that the death has occurred. Then both will hurt deeply and need to begin active mourning. But often it will be the man who must deal with making the funeral arrangements, seeing to all the other practical problems that arise, and providing a public shoulder for his wife to lean on, an arm to grasp, a hand to hold.

When there are relatives to be informed by telephone, often the man makes these calls. If no one has offered to meet planes, trains, or buses, or if there is a need for a family member to do so, he is usually the one who goes.

The man is often asked how his *wife* is holding up, how *she* is doing, how *she* is taking it. The man may be yelling inside, "*I'm* not holding up, *I'm* not doing well, *I'm* not taking it. When is my time to mourn?" But rarely does anyone ask about him, especially if he gives the appearance of being "together."

So the man enters the period I call "functioning robot," packing unreleased feeling upon unreleased feeling inside of him. He turns on his computer, as it were, each morning and functions throughout the day as programmed. He's too busy to mourn—or so he may tell himself.

Eventually, he may take an extra week or so from work, ready to begin active mourning. Usually he now has to play catch-up with his wife in this process, and has to return to work *far* before its completion; but at least he has begun active mourning, and it is truly better late than never.

But more severe mourning problems can occur when the man tries to continue as a functioning robot without any kind of break, when he tries to override the hurt of mourning and return directly to equilibrium. It *never* works, and it can wreak long-term or permanent damage. This behavior is not preplanned. As a matter of fact, the man is trying to do what is "right," to be a supportive, good, strong husband.

But by the time he thinks he has fulfilled that role, the wake is over, the funeral is over, the after-funeral details have been taken care of, the relatives have gone home, and nobody but his wife seems to be talking about the death any more. And her talking may not include a "listening" component for her husband's feelings.

He can't very well start active, ongoing mourning now, he reasons; it is just about over. Somehow he missed it. So better to try to go on. If absolutely necessary, he can mourn quietly by himself in a compartment of life here or there.

And everyone lets him do just that. No one stops him, sits him down, gives him a punching bag and some handkerchiefs and says, "Okay, pal, now it's your turn." (I wish boxing gloves, punching bags, and sweat suits would become as acceptable as tributes of sympathy as are flowers and charitable donations.)

The statistics of severely wounded or broken marriages surrounding the death of a child are very high. And often it is because husbands and wives do not develop a regular pattern of communication, because they mourn at different paces, or because the woman is free to go through active mourning while the man, thinking he must be the strong, functioning member of the family, tries to postpone his mourning or override it completely.

The most important thing for mourning couples to know is that in virtually all marriages, good as well as not-so-good, husbands and wives cannot consistently be each other's sole or even primary comforter. Wives, if you expect your husbands to be rocks throughout the death of your child, or other tragedy in which you both mourn, you are asking too much of them. And you are, without meaning to, cheating them out of their chance to engage in active mourning. Husbands, if you expect your wives to recognize your need to mourn actively and give you permission to do so, you are asking too much of them. You will have to take control of your own mourning, by claiming time and space to do it.

This can be a no-win situation. The husband functions as a robot waiting for permission to begin active mourning, waiting for his turn to mourn. And the wife does not give that permission because she continues to need the husband to take charge and give comfort—or simply doesn't notice his need. He cannot provide all the comfort she needs because he is functioning as a robot. The cycle is self-defeating.

Soon the wife is feeling her husband is not giving her any comfort at all any more; and the husband, trying to compartmentalize, override, or ignore active mourning because he now feels it's too late, is working frantically to return to something resembling daily life before the tragedy.

Not always, but often, the husband wants sex, seeing it as a way of returning to normalcy. He feels as if he will be in control again with sex. He considers sex life-affirming in the face of death. And, perhaps above all he *feels* something when he's having sex. In fact, he may find that sex is the *only* release he can get for all the emotions held captive in him. The need for sex with his wife can almost take possession of him.

But the mother of a recently deceased child may be horrified by the thought. She is not yet ready to return to a normal sex life. She remembers that sex was where the baby started, and the baby is now dead. She is afraid of the reminder. She is afraid of pregnancy and a repeat death. The need not to have sex can be as much an obsession with the wife as the need to do so is for the husband.

This is not true for all women. At times a renewed sexual relationship, if approached with gentleness and mutual understanding, can have an equally rejuvenating effect on both husband and wife. But when husband and wife are profoundly at odds on the issue of resuming sexual relations, professional help may be the only answer.

Professional help is often crucial for a husband and wife having difficulty mourning the death of a child, regardless of whether the difficulty is expressed as a disagreement about sex. The help of friends can benefit greatly. And, at times the help of friends can even make the difference in whether or not the couple gets through the mourning process intact. But this is rare. *Usually a couple mourning the death of their child will feel better if they get some form of professional help from the beginning*.

At best, this professional help will provide an ongoing, regular and neutral *communication resource* for the couple during the mourning process. In one instance, a couple was given "homework" by the therapist to talk together about their child's death for ten minutes every day.

Regardless of the form of communication, however, it is vital that it exist and be ongoing if a marriage is to survive intact and in strength through the death of a child.

At children's hospitals, social workers, psychologists, chaplains, and nurses and doctors often have the names of professionals who can help; or at least they can steer a couple in the right direction. Sometimes you may be most helpful to your friends mourning the dying or death of their child by encouraging them to get such help.

Often a couple will not seek professional help because they are afraid it will appear to their friends that their marriage isn't strong. As their friend you can let them know that the death of a child is a nightmare beyond the expectations of any marriage, no matter how wonderful; and that getting help is a way of saying that their marriage is too valuable to take risks. Help them know that getting temporary support is a way of saying that they love each other and know that both loved the child so much that neither could expect the other to be a tower of strength during this nightmare.

Give your friends who are mourning the death of their child permission to get professional help, aid in finding it if necessary, and support while they are receiving it. The same can be said for *any* friend who is having trouble entering or completing active mourning and moving toward new equilibrium and incorporation. In many cases this professional help is free or low-cost, so there is no reason for anyone who can benefit not to receive it.

Another thing that can help couples mourning the death of a child or others in mourning, is participation in a group of their peers in mourning. There are a number of such groups throughout the country. Those for parents include Candlelighters, Compassionate Friends, and SIDS (for parents of children who died of Sudden Infant Death Syndrome), to name a few. Again, hospital social work, psychology, nursing or chaplaincy departments should have names of support groups in your area. If your friends in mourning haven't heard of these, you could get information for them and encourage them to attend. Groups are very understanding of the newcomer's reluctance to be there.

Another thing to remember about the traditional father in mourning. In situations where a child is given a terminal diagnosis a number of months before the death occurs, the father in many cases *remains in shock from the moment he hears the diagnosis until the final stages of dying*. This is especially true if the child is able to be home and reasonably active during much of this time, and if the man is achievement-oriented in his work.

Such a man expects himself to be able to provide for his family, to give them security, and protect them from harm. He does this by being successful in his job, paying for as comfortable a home as possible in as safe a neighborhood as possible. And when he is told his child will die he cannot accept it.

All this time the father has been provider and protector. He will continue. He works harder and harder, for it is his job that provides the means for security and protection. He can control his job, so logically he can control security and protection also. He will, in a literal sense, "work" to keep his ill child alive. When the ill child is at home and reasonably active, it is a sign that the father is winning the battle, so he tries to keep the child more active to prove that she is strong. He suggests active family play and outings, and his child often will exert great effort to participate in these activities because she wants to please her father.

Such family outings can reap rewards. Assuming the child does "make it" through the outing, she feels a sense of accomplishment and the family has a memory which, though bittersweet, is nonetheless one of happy togetherness.

When the child must re-enter the hospital, the father uses this time to work even harder. He visits regularly, but briefly, and hears only the good news. If there is little or no good news he asks only when the child can come home again.

Thus goes the cycle: not numb shock and not holding onto hope, but *active denial*. The social words may say "holding on to hope;" the activity may imply bargaining; but the fact is denial.

The mother, on the other hand, has begun to go through the process of anticipatory mourning. She has been in the denial and numbness of shock. But then she begins to release anger, weep, become frightened, feel guilty, bargain, feel physical pain, and go into and out of depression and hope.

With the wife engaging in some forms of preliminary mourning and the husband in active shock-denial, often neither reaches what Dr. Kubler-Ross calls "acceptance" before the death.

This difference between husband and wife in dealing with the child's dying can strain the marriage. The husband is striving for ongoing, normal life as a family. The wife is willing to act this out at times but resists it at others; she also needs comforting and strength of a nature that is not now within the husband's power to give. He is using all available energy to deny death.

Before the child dies, however, neither parent may allow their problem to reach the surface beyond a moment here and there. Because in whatever ways they are working, both are genuinely directing all their energies toward the ill child.

"Why argue over trivial matters when my child is dying," the mother will think.

"I won't argue with her about this now; it can wait until all of this is over," the father thinks, not acknowledging to himself that "over" could mean anything but the family remaining whole.

When the child comes very close to death, the father can no longer actively deny her illness. At this time he may go through an entire anticipatory mourning process in a short time—anger, guilt, bargaining, pain, fear, depression, and even tears all in a matter of hours or days. But the wife may not be aware of what he is experiencing, since often a man will do his mourning at the office, in private behind a closed door, on a jogging path, in a steam room, or in a bar. He usually mourns alone, or with a close friend (with whom he will talk around his feelings at best, while trying to drown them at the surface).

Regardless of whether or not the father goes through this preliminary mourning process as the child's death approaches, he will end up back in shock as the death is happening. It will be a shock in which he can no longer deny the fact that his child is ill, and in which he now is trying to accept the fact that the child is dying. It is no longer active denial, but it is not belief either.

In the meantime, hit with the imminence of death, no matter what kind of preliminary mourning she may have engaged in, the wife has returned to being in shock, so that husband and wife are now in a similar state.

Because they are now reacting similarly, the husband and wife may go through the last stages of their child's dying together, offering each other support, space, and closeness. In their state of shock, they can discuss practical matters, make arrangements, and relive memories. It may be the only time during the process that they can be this close.

The child dies. The fact is accepted. The parents see the

child's dead body and at some point belief will follow. But it is likely that they will then strike out again on different paths of mourning.

What can you do to help these parents between the diagnosis and the death? Maybe not much more than listen, and even that won't always help a great deal. The husband will rarely if ever talk realistically about the situation. The wife will talk a great deal in any preliminary mourning she is doing; and if you can, listen, and keep the door of comfort ajar, much as you would with someone in mourning after death.

But don't expect your listening to help as much at this time as it may after the death. It will help, but the wife most of all wants to say these things to her husband, and have him be understanding and hold and soothe, and comfort her, which he cannot do since he is out slaying the dragon. When the dragon attacks the village, the knight first slays the dragon and then comforts fair maiden.

If you can find a professional on the hospital staff who knows the family, you might mention your concern. The professional may then try to meet with the parents individually or together, to talk to them about what they are going through, why they are out of sync with each other, and why that is often the case with husbands and wives in such circumstances.

If they do consult a professional, it is possible only the mother will be able to hear. And chances are still minimal that either parent can take action to change anything at the moment. However, in time they may remember this meeting, and once the child has died, they may better understand each other in mourning, or feel more comfortable seeking help from a professional.

Another way you may be of great help to your friends is by doing something for any siblings of the dying or dead child. It is often the case, though this certainly is not intentional on the parents' part, that when a child has a terminal illness, the sibling is neglected. He doesn't appear to them to need attention because he's healthy. The parents may even actively avoid him because simply by living, he may be a subconscious reminder to them of what the ill or dead child can never be.

The sibling's need in comparison with the needs of an ill child may be minimized or put on a shelf because the parents assume there will be plenty of time to deal with them later.

But this can be a time of acute misery for him. He may not

adequately understand what is happening to the ill child and no one may have taken the time to explain it to him. He may be frightened by the illness, and may feel lonely, especially if he and the sick child are close in age and used to be playmates.

The ill child will receive cards and gifts, especially when in the hospital, and this can make the well child feel neglected or unloved. He may even wish himself ill or display symptoms of illness in order to gain attention.

His parents will often be tired or distracted. This may be especially true of his mother, who was probably the one who met most of his daily needs. The sibling may well feel that no one cares about him any more.

These and other feelings can often lead him to perform less well in school, retreat to his room or to the home of friends, or act out.

As a friend, there may be several things you can do to help the child, and thereby help his parents. If possible, you can give him some attention. Often the parents will be pleased to have some of his needs met by someone else occasionally. And when you ask permission to take the child out—anything from a walk to a weekend—it may give them a gentle reminder that they should give him some time, too, when possible.

If you have children, explain to them briefly what you are trying to do, and enlist their cooperation and understanding. If you have no children, that is not a reason not to go on an outing with the child. Children are rarely singled out to go somewhere with an adult, and, at best, a child may feel honored and special to be asked; alternately, he may simply be so desperate to be with someone who can give him a few hours of undivided attention that he will go, even with an adult he may not know that well. However, in order for him to feel comfortable and safe, he usually has to feel his parents know and like you.

The child may not talk much; or he may talk non-stop. Be prepared for either. But let him talk about himself, not only about his ill or dead sibling (unless it's in relation to his own feelings).

Depending on circumstances, start slowly and pace the number of outings you take with the child. Don't commit to taking Johnny to the movie every Saturday during his sibling's dying process unless you're prepared to do so for months or even years. Dying can take a long time. And don't promise to do anything unless you're as sure as possible that you will be able to do it. Remember the length of the child's memory where positive promises are concerned. If you cannot do something you promised, explain why to the child himself, rather than leave a message, unless unavoidable.

Any person-to-person attention you can give on a reasonably regular basis to the sibling of a terminally ill or recently dead child will benefit both the sibling and his parents. But don't ever openly criticize the sibling's parents for neglecting him. Give them a boost by helping him know his parents love him deeply.

If you can't give personal attention to the sibling of a terminally ill child, you can still remember him. When asking about the ill child, remember to ask about the sibling, too. When sending a card to the ill child, remember occasionally to send a "Hi" card to the well child. When buying a gift for the ill child, remember occasionally to bring along something for the sibling.

If you call the home, talk with the sibling for a while if he answers the phone, asking how he is and what is is doing, before asking to speak to the parents or the ill child.

If there is a school activity which his parents would normally attend but cannot, offer to go and represent them. Visit all the sibling's classes; go to Parents' Day or PTA; cheer him and his team on if it's a sports activity. He'll be pleased to have an adult supporting him; it will make him feel more like his peers.

For siblings feel "different" when their brother or sister is dying or has died. Many of their friends may be afraid that whatever the ill child has is catching through the well child and, out of fear that what is happening to the ill child could happen to them or their sibling, they may avoid their friend. The well child may be acting differently, too, which makes his friends all the more uneasy about how to treat him or what to say. This, at its worse, can result in teasing or taunting. Children not guided by sympathetic parents or teachers can be terribly cruel.

And, finally, if you discover that the well child really doesn't understand what is happening to his sibling, you may discuss with his parents the possibility of a visit to the hospital so that he can see. This has proven very therapeutic in helping children come to grips with serious illness and the approach of death.

It can also help friends of the ill child if they, too, can visit the hospital. Not all children want a spotlight on their illness, however, so visits and activities should depend on the personality and feelings of the ill child.

Being a friend to the family of a terminally ill child is difficult; but it can be extremely helpful in the long run, especially as the mourning process continues after death. While the child was dying you may have sensed that there was very little you could do that would make the parents feel better. And you were right, because the only help the parents really wanted was a cure for the illness, and understanding and support from each other. However, after the child dies, it is likely that the parents will remember that you were there during the journey, sharing in their grief. This may make them feel closer to you during the ultimate mourning process than they would if you had withdrawn prior to their child's death.

6

Dying

THE PRIMARY PURPOSE of this book is to discuss ways in which one can be a friend to someone who is mourning the death of a person she loves. If, however, it is your friend who is dying, she will be mourning the approaching loss of her "self."

Dr. Kubler-Ross first defined this mourning process by dividing it into stages: shock and isolation, anger, bargaining, depression, and acceptance. It is helpful to know that these are feelings that your friend may be dealing with during the process of her dying; but don't feel you need to know what stage your friend has reached every time you see or talk to her.

If you are very close to someone who is dying, you will likely feel some of the same emotions of mourning that she is experiencing, though not necessarily at the same time. This preliminary mourning is normal for both of you. Both of you are in the process of losing someone you love—your friend—and of losing something you love—your special relationship.

I used to think that if I knew I had only one year to live I would want to travel to the far reaches of the earth and then die in Paris overlooking Notre Dame. But probably I would do none of this, except for perhaps a last nostalgic trip to Paris. Chances are that I would stay where I am and keep working at a job I love. I would want to continue to be with my family and close friends, keep on living my normal life as long as possible and in every way possible. This is because the things of value in my life are my family, and friends, and job; and those things are not at the far reaches of the earth.

It is the things of greatest value, usually the intangibles of love and friendship and pride in work, that a person wants to hold on to, to treasure, when she knows she will soon die. It is difficult enough to try to fathom that friendships and love as we know them in our daily lives on earth must one day end. It is even more unfathomable to think that they might end before death. For this reason, many people with terminal illnesses want to keep their lives as normal as possible. But a person with a diagnosed terminal illness will never be able to keep her life the same as it was before the diagnosis. The old equilibrium is gone. The old self is gone, and the new self includes the diagnosis— "terminal."

This is very frightening, not only to the person with the diagnosis, but to her family and friends. And so begins a tug of war between trying to keep things normal, and acknowledging that Oh, God, someone loved is dying. Nevermore begins to loom.

The person who is dying is likely to have many actively concerned friends at the beginning and end of her illness—her "coming-out" and her "going-out." Most terminal diagnoses come as a result of medical tests and procedures done during a hospitalization. Since friends visit friends when they are hospitalized, if a terminal diagnosis is made at that time, the news generally gets out, and family and friends, and the patient herself (unless she has requested otherwise), soon know the verdict. This brings an influx of phone calls, visitors, and notes, and many offers of "If I can do anything, let me know."

But many well-meaning people, both relatives and friends, are afraid of not knowing what to do or say, afraid of doing or saying the wrong things, and/or afraid in a strange but human way of coming too close to the terminal illness and catching it. So after initial contact they drift away from the person with the terminal diagnosis, or at best see her in groups, where no one person has to feel responsible for keeping a conversation going.

As the person with the terminal diagnosis nears death, however, these people return. Wanting to have done more all along, they now get up their courage and visit for one last time to say good-bye.

They try to do this while the patient is lucid so she will know they cared. Relieved and feeling less guilty, they can then say they saw their friend just before she died.

I offer no condemnation of this. It is the normal human pattern. It has been my pattern more than once, so I know it well.

But at times people do want to do more, say more, or be more with someone who is dying. What, then can help? Here are some thoughts on listening, talking, doing, and touching.

LISTENING

Listening is active. Listening is not time spent daydreaming or thinking about what you're going to say next or wishing the speaker would hurry up and finish so you can talk; true listening is active participation with the other person in what he is saying. We participate by keeping our mouths shut, and our minds on our friend's words and their meanings, on his speech tone and pattern, on what may be implied, and on what may be left unsaid. This is active work. And it is hard work, which may leave you exhausted.

But truly trying our best to hear what a person is saying to us is one of the most valuable ways we can show the person that we love him, for it shows we respect him enough to give our time to try to hear who he is. My guess is that the single greatest reason for unhappy marriages and love relationships is that people either do not want or know how to actively listen to each other, and are not willing to work at it. The need of one or both partners to dwell on themselves, on the importance of their thoughts and ideas, is simply too great.

If you can do no more than actively listen to your friend who is dying, you very probably will have done the thing that matters most. Often people who are dying are filibustered by people who mean well, but who are so afraid that the subject of death will come up that they just talk non-stop at the person. Therefore, people who are dying often have few people who will listen to them other than professionals they meet as a result of their illness—people like hospital social workers, psychologists, nurses, and/or chaplains.

Ideally we professionals are good listeners. But we do not know your friend as you have known him, *before his illness*. It is you who will understand more what he faces losing—his history—for you have lived some or much of it with him. When he talks about the joy of something past we can share in his mourning, but we can't share in his memories. You can.

In order for you to listen, your friend has to talk. This may not happen overnight. Like the child frightened by the unknown power of his feelings of mourning, your friend is feeling threatened by the unknown power of his dying. Not only is he scared to think that he will die, that he will be on earth no more, he also is scared to think what that dying will feel like.

Will there be disfigurement? Will there be horrible pain? Will there be odor? Will he lose control of bodily functions and be embarrassed? Will he lose control mentally? Will he lose hair or eyesight? Will he lose all dignity? Will he not be brave? Will he lose hope? Will he be alone?

To unleash all of these frightening questions at once is too threatening. So like the child moving through the unknown realm of mourning, your friend, moving through the unknown realm of dying, tries to compartmentalize his feelings, especially in the beginning. During this time he will be testing his own ability to integrate his diagnosis into his life, and at some level he will be testing the stamina of his family and friends.

Many relatives and friends of someone with a terminal illness, in order to try to cope with the loss themselves, bury their friend with the diagnosis. In long-term illness this is very frustrating to the person who isn't dead yet.

He has precious little time as it is and, given support and encouragement from his family and friends—like you—he will still want to *live* that time. He can be talked into doing a number of things if he feels genuinely wanted.

If he thinks his relatives and friends are seeing him dead all the time, that's how he'll see himself. But if he thinks they are seeing him as alive and wanted and needed, then that's how he'll see himself, too, more often than not.

In listening to your terminally ill friend you don't have to worry bout *what* to listen for at first. Your friend will be in shock for a while and may be talking a great deal about the data of his diagnosis to several family members and friends. He will be trying to accept that data as fact. He won't yet *believe* he is actually dying, and may not for some time. He may not even believe the diagnosis for a while, until invasive procedures or therapies that somehow change him begin to take place. And even this initial belief may recede if he goes into a full remission. But at least he will be talking enough to try to integrate the data into his mind as a statement of fact.

Pacing is very important to being a listening friend to someone who is dying. The length and intensity of terminal illness are not predictable. If you try to smother your friend with attention in the beginning, both of you may weary before the journey is done; or you may set up false expectations you find you can't live up to in the long haul.

So if active listening is what you feel you can offer, start slowly and be where your friend is. Begin to listen for when he wants to talk about something serious, when he wants to talk about ordinary things, when he wants to vent frustrations, when he wants to be happy, and when he doesn't want to talk at all.

Listening, when it is active and when the shadow of nevermore looms, can be physically as well as emotionally exhausting. I can come home after a day of work and hurt from the marrow of my bones out, yet I may have done nothing more "physical" than walk between patient rooms one or two times per hour all day. When you are a true listening friend to your friend who is dying, know that it may leave you physically as well as emotionally exhausted.

Remember, too, that it takes time to develop your listening skills and, at times, even the professional misses the mark. *So go slowly.* Just as in helping a friend mourn the death of someone he loves, keep the door of communication ajar.

Notes and cards keep this door open at times, as do telephone calls and visits. When you call, ask if you are interrupting anything, or if it's a bad time. And when you want to visit, call ahead and offer several options.

By slowly and surely opening the door of communication and keeping it ajar, you are letting your friend know that you intend to be there for him for the duration. In time, new trust in your ability to live out the illness together will be built and incorporated into the previous relationship. And your friend will know that he can count on you when he needs someone to really listen.

What may your friend talk to you about?

Hope.

Throughout his illness, your friend will probably continue to hope most of the time, and he will want you and others who care about him to do so as well. At first the hope may be for a mistaken diagnosis, then for a complete remission, then for a miracle drug, then for no drug side effects, then for his hair to stay. He may hope for a miracle healing, then for a long remission, then for a remission, then for no pain, then for less pain. Finally he may hope for an accepting outlook, then to die peacefully with those he loves near, then for happy lives for those who remain.

If your friend is religious or has found a form of faith during his illness, which often happens and about which no one should be judgmental, he may also talk with you about hope for a life hereafter. There are enough studies now of "near-death" experiences of light and peace and beauty and being met by someone who died before, that theories of life after death may give even cynics pause. To one who has faith, great peace in dying can come in the belief that we die only to this world but not to eternity.

I personally believe that is so, and try to help patients consider that possibility if they are open to it, even if they have had little or no faith before.

If your friend has little faith but seems to want to think about such things now, you can help him most, perhaps, by letting him know he isn't being a hypocrite. (Concern about being hypocritical is what I hear most from previously unbelieving patients.) *If you believe and are comfortable,* help him see that God's love is a constant, that there is no computer tote board in the sky. And, ask if this is really a time to worry about how things "look"—especially when God isn't worrying!

Then, back off. Give him time to think. *DON'T PUSH.* Don't shower him with Bibles or religious tracts unless requested. Just keep the door ajar for talk of faith. God will do the rest.

If your friend already believes in the hereafter, give him room to talk about it and be happy and anticipatory with him if that's how he's feeling. When you're dying, thinking of life hereafter is *not* morbid. It is a joy.

But regardless of which "hope" your friend is discussing with you, it *is* hope. And you can hope with your friend, whether it be for no pain or for a miracle.

In the case of a miracle, hoping with is different from promising or giving false hope. It is simply agreeing with the friend you love that it would be good if he could be well. And a lot of healing comes with love. He will know you care enough to hope with him for what he wants for himself, without needing to introduce statistics and laws of averages into the picture. He almost certainly knows those statistics just as well as you do, and if he doesn't want to talk about them, there's no reason for you to.

If your friend hopes for a miracle to the neglect of things that could help his healing or slow the progression of his illness, that is a different matter. You can let him know that you hope for a miracle for him, too; but in the meantime you would encourage him to use the benefits of medical science (unless, as a Christian Scientist, he is choosing not to) to keep him more comfortable until such a miracle should occur.

This situation rarely happens. Most non–Christian Scientists use the tools of medical science where appropriate and thera-peutic, and continue to hope for healing at the same time. Some people choose to reject major treatment, such as chemotherapy; and that is their right. But ideally they do not make such a choice because they expect a miracle healing of the flesh.

There is a sad joke about such a situation, but it does make a good point:

A man is in his home and a flood comes. An evacuation truck comes by. "No," says the man, "I'll stay here. God won't let anything happen to me." The water swells and the man goes to the second floor of his home. A person comes by in a boat to rescue him. "No," says the man, "I'll stay here. God won't let anything happen to me." The water rises far-ther. The man goes up to his roof and a person comes by in a helicopter to rescue him. "No," says the man, "I'll stay here. God won't let anything happen to me." Soon the flood waters engulf the house and the man drowns. When he gets to heaven, he is soaked and furious. "I trusted you com-pletely, God," he fumes, "why didn't you rescue me?" God replies, "I sent you a truck, a boat, and a helicopter; what more did you want?"

Anger is another thing your friend may talk to you about. It may be anger at God, who he believes is causing or allowing him to suffer and die. It may be anger at relatives or other friends for not being all he feels they could be for him now, or for gossiping about him and his illness behind his back, or for abandoning him. It may be anger at the medical staff—though usually not his primary physician as long as he or she is offering some form of treatment. It may be anger at the regular complexities and red tape of living, now magnified by his situation. Or it may simply be anger for anger's sake, a need to express rage at his lack of control over what is happening to him.

But as mentioned earlier, anger takes so much energy that it exhausts itself. It will feed on itself for a time until the emotion is spent; but then it wearies. In the meantime, just listen without being judgmental.

At times we assume all anger coming from a terminally ill person is because he is dying. But your friend may be angry for perfectly ordinary, concrete reasons, either a reason having nothing to do with his illness (and not blown out of proportion because of it), or a reason that does have to do with his illness but is, nonetheless, a very specific response to a particular situation.

For example, after undergoing scores of invasive procedures, blood tests, biopsies, etc., a technician makes a mistake and your friend has to have an unnecessary repeat procedure. This happens, and it can be reason for anger when one has been a medical pincushion for weeks. It's important to listen to the specifics of your friend's anger, and not just utter soothing bromides about how you understand his feelings. Give your friend room and support to express anger at regular, ordinary mishaps; that is an anger you can often share more readily than a general anger at fate.

Another thing your friend may talk to you about is guilt.

He may feel guilty about his angers, especially any anger at family and friends and God. Let him know these angers are normal.

In the Christian faith, Jesus was angered and saddened when His friends fell asleep after He asked them to wait with Him while He prayed in the garden, only hours before His death. But Jesus knew they were still His friends, just human. *And He did need and want them.* He didn't choose to face His dying alone.

Jesus got angry in frustration on the cross, too. "My God, my God, why hast Thou forsaken me?" Even Jesus questioned God when He felt alone and abandoned.

If your friend is a Christian, these reminders may help him

know his feelings are normal, and justified by God Himself incarnate in a suffering, and dying, and very human Jesus Christ.

Your friend also may tell you he feels guilty for abandoning his family by dying. This, too, is normal, especially if he fears for the family's financial security, that their daily needs won't be met. Let your friend know that his feelings are normal. (If you can and are willing to help in this sensitive financial area, let him know you will.)

Ongoing daily faith is another major area about which your friend may wish to talk. Perhaps his strong faith is holding him together. He may want to speak to this. He may even want to encourage you to have more faith. Don't feel you have to say or feel things you don't believe because of this, but listen and respect his need to talk to you about these things as a sign he cares about you.

He may also be testing his traditional faith. He may feel hurt by God because he has tried to live a good life and now has a terminal illness as his so-called reward. Sometimes there is nothing you can do to help with that pain but listen, and listening may do very little good.

I had a patient I loved very dearly who was diagnosed as having cancer the day after he retired. When he was admitted to the Rehabilitation Institute most but not all of his spinal cord tumor had been surgically removed, leaving him with paralysis from the waist down.

The man's physician asked me to see him because he seemed increasingly withdrawn and depressed, but would never discuss this or any other feeling issues related to his illness.

Mr. Janeau was a solidly built, gray-haired man who spent a great amount of time reading, especially newspapers. In my first few visits with him, Mr. Janeau insisted he was fine. He would invite me to sit down, but would keep his newspaper half open in an attempt to keep the visit casual. I followed his lead and didn't push, and in time he folded the newspaper and put it away when I arrived.

Slowly he told me about his life. Just before his tumor was discovered he had sold the neighborhood bar that he had owned and personally run as bartender all his adult life. He and his wife had planned to travel to Italy to see his ancestral home. Mr. and Mrs. Janeau had been married over forty years and had raised three children, all of whom were married, with families, and living in various parts of the country. The family was close despite the distance of miles.

Mr. Janeau told me that his grandfather had deserted his grandmother, and his father had deserted his mother. He told me that his grandmother and mother had worked very hard to raise their children alone. Mr. Janeau said that early in his life he swore he would never desert his wife, and that he would work hard at an honest living and worship in the Catholic church regularly, all to honor the memory of his grandmother and mother, and to break the pattern of his father's and grandfather's behavior.

With no self-righteousness, but with quiet pride, Mr. Janeau said he had, as best he could, fulfilled this vow to himself and to God. But it was here in the conversation, on the several occasions the topic arose, that Mr. Janeau would look away from me and his eyes would mist.

It took a long time of patient waiting and a deep and real trust before this quiet, large, self-made man of deep faith would admit, with tears running down his face, that he was hurt by God and that he really didn't understand. He didn't understand why, when his father and grandfather lived such irresponsible, irreligious lives and he had tried so hard to live a steady, ethical, and faithful life, that God would let his ancestors live to healthy, ripe old ages and would give him this "problem" that paralyzed him and prevented him from enjoying a retirement of travelling with his wife. It didn't seem fair to him. Mr. Janeau was hurt by God and deep inside angry in human helplessness with God.

About two years after his rehab stay, Mr. Janeau died a very painful death. He never walked again, he never visited Italy. And though he gave me the Bible that I carried on my wedding day, he never really got over his hurt and anger with God.

Sometimes, though faith may falter, it eventually is revived and renewed. Often people test their traditional faith, find it to have holes, mend those holes, and ultimately find a stronger faith. If your friend is testing his faith, listen to his feelings without judgment.

If your friend says prayer and worship are becoming more difficult for him, this can be a sign of anger or hurt with God. A child suffering a fate he doesn't understand and thinking his parent is responsible for it may stomp off saying, "I'll never speak to you again." It is the child's way of paying the parent back, the only revenge he feels he has the power to exert. So it is, at least on a subconscious level, that your friend may be trying to "pay God back." This is between your friend and God. Listening without judgment is often all you can do.

Even if you are not of the same faith as your friend, it cannot hurt to let him know that you are interested in his feelings about faith. People are often reluctant to talk openly about these issues, especially in the face of terminal illness, for fear of "turning off" their friends. If given permission, your friend may truly welcome the opportunity to talk about something he fears no one else will want to hear.

TALKING

You may have noticed that you've begun to do some talking. Active listening at times demands only silence; at other times it may demand response. But if you have been listening actively, response will not be as difficult. You'll usually know the helpful thing to say in the moment, and usually it will be more right than you suspect.

If you are stymied, however, I offer a few simple suggestions. If a question comes somewhat out of the blue, like "What do you think of suicide?"—to mention a blockbuster that could stun even the closest, most attentive of friends; though it is with such a friend that this question most often is posed—what your friend may really be saying is "I've been wondering what *I* think of suicide under the circumstances." So ask her.

You can say something like "Why do you ask?" or "What would make you think about that?" That is not saying that you won't answer her question, but it is asking for more background to her thinking before you respond. That's probably all you will have to say for a while, because your friend will have gotten the opening she wanted, and will start talking.

If you are pushed for an opinion, you can agree in a general sense with whatever she is thinking *as long as it does not conflict with your beliefs or demand complicity or permission from you in any actual suicide*. If it does conflict with your beliefs, you can say so. But be sure to label them as your beliefs and not as ones which are absolute or held by everyone in the world. If your friend asks complicity, giving it is a crime and you should be aware of that. If your friend asks permission, that is your choice. Just be sure you can live with whatever you say. It is usually wiser not to be caught up in either giving or denying permission in discussions of suicide contemplated by someone terminally ill.

A word about suicide. Don't be judgmental or shocked unless you have walked in your friend's shoes. Unless you are his priest and it is a question of doctrine, suicide is a matter between a person and God. We are not our brother's *judge* in matters such as that. Many decent people have opted for suicide in the face of an unknown or frightening future on earth. People who have valid reason to foresee only pain, dependence, and/or suffering here have taken their own lives in hope and not in despair; in hope that there is something better coming, even if, in their minds, that something better is mere nothingness.

If your terminally ill friend talks to you about suicide, hear her out. Let her know you love her and care about her and don't want to lose her.

Don't make promises you can't keep. Just let her know that you will continue to be her friend throughout.

Even if the discussion of suicide seems strictly philosophical, not practical, you may wish to ask certain questions.

Ask her if she has thought of how she would act out the suicide. Does she have a plan?

Ask her to wait if you feel she may plan to act on these thoughts soon. Ask her to think on it and sleep on it more.

Ask her if she has talked with anyone else about this. If not, tell her you feel you must mention this discussion to at least one other person, perhaps a family member, a member of the clergy, or her primary physician. This takes the sole burden of knowledge from you.

And ask her if she it talking of suicide because of great pain, or because she fears dying alone or being a care burden to her family and friends. If this is so, then you may be of great help to her and her family by putting them in touch with a hospice if there is one in your area.

Hospices are designed for people with terminal illness, helping them to stay at home with support care as long as feasible, after which they are admitted to the hospice facility, where specially trained staff administer to their needs with care and understanding. Hospices offer medical and emotional support to the dying and to their families. And members of a hospice medical team are usually trained in administering pain medication for optimum legal results.

There are those who feel that the U.S. could legalize, *for pain control in terminal illness only*, the use of currently controlled or banned substances that, properly administered, would ease severe pain more effectively than substances now in use. One such group is the National Committee on the Treatment of Intractable Pain, P.O. Box 9553, Friendship Station, Washington, D.C. 20016-1553.

If your friend is considering suicide because she fears increasing pain, dying alone, or being a burden on her family, a hospice program could make all the difference. Another thing that could ease her mind about being allowed to die with dignity, and without implicating her family in morally problematic decision-making, is a document called the living will. Now legal in a number of states, it states that the person signing it does not wish heroic procedures to be used when her death is *inevitable*. This lightens the burden of decision on the family, and frees medical personnel to make decisions about care without fear of malpractice suits. (More information on Living Wills can be obtained by writing Concern for Dying, 250 W. 57th St., New York, N.Y. 10107.)

Perhaps there are guidelines beyond what I have offered. But I feel less than honest offering any more here. Suicide in terminal illness is a very individual matter. The most important thing to remember is that, regardless of her decision, *it is her decision. It is never your fault*; and don't ever let anyone put that blame or burden on you. Suicide is the decision of the person who commits it; no one else shares responsibility for it.

But what about other forms of talking with your friend?

Don't feel you can't talk about the future. Your friend may still have strong views that the Chicago Cubs will win the World Series! She may want to talk about politics, or sports, or think of future vacations and plans, even though she knows she may not be around for them. It's all right. Just enjoy each other. We all talk about a number of future things we never do or see.

She may also want to talk about things she can't do any more but is still interested in, such as a job or gardening. If your friend worked and has had to stop, and if you work where she did, keep her up-to-date on happenings and job scuttlebutt if she seems interested. Not being able to be there doesn't mean not being able to care.

As long as your friend is alive, let her be alive. Terminally ill people can fear increasing isolation almost as much as they fear increasing pain.

She also may want to talk about her will, her death, and her funeral. I've worked around death and dying so long that I have planned not only my funeral, but what I want done with me.

Having a good sense of humor—a necessity in my line of work—I have decided to be cremated and have my ashes divided into eleven containers. Ten friends will take ten small urns, all expenses paid, to ten places I have loved, such as Paris and Coleman Lake, and scatter the ashes. The eleventh urn gets buried. The ten friends, plus a friend or spouse per each of them, have two years to do this so that they can get over any mourning they may do and just have fun on the trip.

Perhaps only people who have worked in the area of death and dying as long as I could have my strange sense of humor. But your friend facing death may well want to discuss that death and her funeral. Allow her. You can say something to let her know that you hope the reason for this discussion is still a far piece away, unless she is in her last days. If so, then just grit your teeth and talk with her about it. Pollyannas are not welcome when an active effort is being made to face death. You will be doing your friend a great favor by allowing her to talk about what now concerns her most.

If the discussion should involve concrete funeral wishes, write them down and let her see you do this, if possible. Then she'll know you won't forget. If it involves your presence at the death-bed, listen, but do not promise absolutely to be with her in the moment of death unless death is imminent and you therefore know you can be there. Otherwise, you could be devastated if unable to keep your promise. Even if your friend didn't know whether or not you were there at the end, you would know, and any failure on your part could bother you for a long time.

So, if you think you can, tell her you will try to be with her—but don't promise.

Finally, your terminally ill friend may want to talk to you about you. She may be sick of talking about herself. She may want to hear what you think and how you feel, and what is going on in your life. She may want for a time to ignore completely that she is or ever was sick and to have a relaxed time with you and talk about you—just as she did in happier times.

This can be problematic for a friend who is sharing a deep listening relationship with the person who is dying, and isn't quite sure of what she wants. She may just want some time of respite; but she may want something more in depth. She may want to know how her approaching death is affecting you, too.

If that is the case, you can tell her it's hard on you—*not the listening to her*, but the fact of her illness. She won't want to think that listening is too much for you, because she needs it too much; but she may need to know that you are suffering with her—not that she wants you to hurt, but that she wants (at times) a sense of sympatico in her journey.

There is one final area of "talking" I want to discuss.

You won't have to make speeches about your support. It will be visible. You won't have to tell the person that you love her or care about her—though a friend saying that *can* be awfully nice at times—because your caring and love will be visible. But there is a speech that you may have to give.

Sometimes a person is so overwhelmed by a terminal diagnosis that if her family and friends don't bury her with it, she will begin to bury herself with it. As belief that she is dying hits her, the person thinks she is no longer effective or desirable or capable—especially as a wife and mother and friend. In most if not all cases that feeling is unfounded.

If you see this happening to your friend, it may be time for a speech. It may be time to sit down with her in a quiet place and help her take her dying by the reins and ride it out "in style."

Point out the qualities in her that are exceptional, that are peculiarly hers, and that will never be lost. They can be sources of courage for her when times get rough.

This is not meant to burden her with unreal expectations of heroic performance. Be sure she understands this. But it is meant to help her see, through the maze of death data now engulfing her, that those qualities that make her who she is are still alive, and can be relied on to get her through.

Don't rush through this speech. Give her time to think about it and integrate it. Look her in the eyes and let her feel your belief in her.

I remember a quote by Senator Jacob Javits, who battled ALS (a progressive muscle-nerve disorder) for over six years before succumbing to it in 1986. "Life does not stop with terminal illness," he said. "Only the patient stops if he doesn't have the will to go forward with life until death overtakes him."

DOING

Doing was discussed in an earlier section on mourning death. Those same things can be helpful at the time a person is dying—cooking, cleaning, transportation, child care, gardening, lawn work, phone-answering, etc. Just keep in mind that your friend may want to do some of the things himself as long as he is able.

If I received a terminal diagnosis on Monday, someone could start cooking for me on Tuesday, and I would probably go out to dinner Monday night. But other things, such as driving, writing, plant-watering, and fishing I would fight to do as long as I could.

Each person has things he loves to do and will try to do as long as possible. The key is, if something looks like it needs to be done—offer. An overgrown lawn, a soiled floor, piles of laundry—approach "with mop in hand." In other words, be convincing. Where you are less certain of need, ask, letting the person know you are available today to do what you can.

You may feel you are not a great listener and that listening is the only important thing anyone can offer. But the most sensitive listener in the world won't hold a candle to you if what your ill friend is worried about that day is a dirty kitchen floor. The quality time that day will be spent by the friend who *listened* to the unspoken plea of a floor that said, "I'm dirty, and the person who owns me is too tired or in too much pain to wash me."

Continuing to do things that are routine between you and your friend—such activities as bowling, cooking classes, golf, or chess—is another way of doing. Your friend may want to continue these activities as long as he is able. Encourage him to do so, and don't forget to include him.

If he is not able to participate actively, he may find it too depressing to watch from the sidelines. But some people like just to be among friends doing familiar things, even when they themselves can no longer join in. Give your friend the opportunity and encouragement to accompany you as long as that's feasible.

Going along without being able to do can be frustrating. But if your friend knows it is all right with his friends and they *want* him any way he can come, it may give him the incentive he needs—and a good time as well.

TOUCHING

We aren't much of a touching society, we Americans, but we certainly and especially avoid touching anything that we think is contaminated or contagious or soiled or ugly. Usually someone who is dying is not dirty or contaminated, contagious, or ugly. But sometimes someone who is in the later stages of dying can exhibit all these unpleasant qualities—and knows it.

A dying person could be bleeding from the mouth or nose or coughing up blood. Blood is not soil, but we often react as if it were. He could have skin disfiguration or openings which secrete. When hospitalized, he could be in a room requiring visitors to put on gowns and gloves and masks before entering. (The visitor may think this is to protect him from catching something from the patient. At times, it is. But more often than not, sterile robings prevent the patient from catching something from the visitor.) And a person with a terminal illness who has lost his hair can at times, in relation to the all-American worship of youth and beauty, feel he is ugly. All of the above may, from the perspective of the ill person or friends, erect a barrier against touching or being touched.

Don't be afraid to touch your friend who has a terminal illness. Except in rare instances, it's not catching. If there is a contagion problem, either from him to you or you to him, follow the necessary precautions. You can still usually touch someone with a gloved hand or kiss your own hand through your facemask and put your hand to his cheek. Even acting out blowing a kiss is better than nothing.

Touching doesn't mean rushing in and hugging the breath out of your dying friend, however. He may be in pain and you won't want to cause more. Touching can be a gentle, simple gesture of taking a hand, touching a cheek, rubbing an arm or shoulder. Sometimes you can be of immeasurable help to a friend by rubbing a painful joint or sore neck. If you feel you want to do this, offer. This may be greatly appreciated. But if pain is too great for physical touching, even a hand or finger next to him on the bed can be something.

I don't minimize the fear of touching, just as I don't minimize the need for touching. I remember well how hard it was for me as a beginning chaplain to enter the rooms of children who didn't look "normal." And when I first did—which happened on the neurosurgery unit where almost no one looked "normal"—I was careful not to touch anything, especially the child!

Finally I bravely touched the side of a crib, then the little hand inside, then a cheek. And soon I was diapering and rocking babies and giving bottles, and even watching dressing changes and surgeries.

Suction machines and great amounts of fluids still get to me at times, but I blur my eyes and try to go on. Someday I may need a suction machine and I hope that someone will hang in there with me. But, of course, that is part of the fear as well. Seeing someone ill reminds us we could be ill that way, too.

When I see someone with mucous, or blood, or a lot of equipment attached, I try to put myself in his place. How would I feel if I were in his place and my friend looked at me as if I were untouchable? Putting myself in another's shoes has helped me through more than once. We never can know how another person feels, but we can try knowing now and then. And, practically speaking, soap and hot water are usually nearby, so that you can always wash your hands if the touching really is a problem for you.

A sensitive friend can help a terminally ill person feel better about himself by not being afraid to touch him, even if there are tubes, or mucous, or blood, or scars, or baldness or an amputation, or whatever. None of us likes to feel ugly. But in the sometimes long battle with terminal illness and its broad spectrum of treatments, one can feel very ugly and untouchable.

By touching your ill friend, you say, "You are beautiful to me, you are not ugly or frightening, you have not become untouchable. You are still a warm and real human being who is valuable to me; you are still my good friend, or my love."

A touch says, "Maybe I cannot say what I feel about you or do what I want to do for you—especially make you well. But I hurt to see you hurt, and I want to touch you even though I know I can't take the hurt away, and even if you cannot touch me back, or grasp my hand, or even feel my touch, I want to say in as many ways as possible that I care."

* * *

Listening, talking, doing, and touching are four ways you can be a friend to someone who is dying.

But what if you feel you don't have the relationship to be, or cannot be a close friend to someone who is dying; but you do want to see him occasionally and are afraid of doing or saying the wrong thing? Here the key is not the amount of time you spend with the ill person, but the quality of the time that you spend.

A friend of mine who is a priest can spend one minute with someone in passing and the person thinks he has talked with the priest for a good five minutes. Another minister friend of mine can spend five minutes with someone and the person thinks the minister has talked with him for only one rushed minute.

The priest stops, stands comfortably or sits, perhaps takes a hand, maintains eye contact, and gives the person the feeling of having his undivided attention and interest. The minister keeps moving, does not sit or relax, does not touch, darts his eyes hither and yon, and gives the person the feeling that he is very busy and doing a favor by even stopping a moment. This, in turn, makes the person uncomfortable and it takes him twice as long to say what he wanted to say because he's feeling guilty for having stopped the minister at all.

Of the two men, the priest is far busier. But the only way one would know it is by the amount of work he does.

When you visit a terminally ill person, you are obviously coming to see him because you like him and are sorry about what he is going through. Bring a gift if you want to, but tell him why you came—not primarily to bring the gift, but to see him and let him know you are sorry that he has to go through all this.

That said he will probably respond. Sit, assuming a chair is offered, relax, look him in the eye, and listen. Don't keep looking at your watch and fidget. He may talk a bit about his situation, or he may just ask about you and/or your family. He's working to make you feel comfortable and he cares about you and your family.

If yours has not been an ongoing and in-depth relationship during the illness, he knows that. He won't suddenly come out with "I'm feeling so angry at God," or "What do you think of suicide?" He will simply enjoy the fact that you cared enough to come and that you seem relaxed in his presence. So answer his questions and respond in kind. Ask about his family. Or address his other interests, maybe sports, or business, or hobbies. Even if he's had to give them up he may enjoy talking about them.

Quality time is calm time, it's active listening time, it's genuinely shared time. It's time that lets the other person know he's important to you. It's time without props for leaning on or gushes of words or filibustering. Quality time does not have to be long, but to be quality time it must be offered in a way that affirms the value of the person you have come to see.

A final note on being a friend to someone who is dying. You may think that to be a good friend to someone who is dying you have to be a family member or an already close friend. That is ideal, but it doesn't always happen that way. *At times, the closer a person is to someone who is dying the more difficult or even impossible he finds it to be close to that person in his process of dying.* The very close family member of your friend may go into shock, denial, and other stages or preliminary mourning so completely that there simply cannot be an ongoing, fulfilling relationship.

Sometimes this problem can be helped by intervention by a disinterested professional. If you see this happening between a friend who is dying and someone very close to him, you may consider suggesting professional help. But sometimes that can be a dead end; either the professional may not be able to help or the defenses of the close friend or family member will be so great that he won't be allowed to try.

So you may become closer to someone who is dying than your relationship previously may have forecast. This happened between a little girl named Taffy and me, and I will tell you about her in a bit.

If you feel you can be a friend to someone who is dying, do it. It won't be easy, for there is even less ''in it'' for a friend who helps someone who is dying than there is for a friend who helps someone in mourning.

After mourning a death, the closely shared relationship between the friends usually returns, sometimes all the stronger. But after going through the dying of a friend, that's it; no new equilibrium; no equilibrium at all. The friend is dead, and you are now the mourner, and he won't be around to return the favor.

Going through a friend's dying with him is a selfless and often intensely painful act. But do it if you can. You may never "know yourself to be so good" again. And somewhere out there is a plain, ordinary human being—not a saint like your dead friend will seem to you to be for a while, but a regular guy—waiting to help you through your mourning. Let him.

DEATH OF A "SINGLE" PERSON

A great many people in this world die alone every day, people without any living relatives, or without relatives who care or are involved. These may be people whose spouses have died, who are divorced, who have no children or whose children are not involved, or who never married and are childless. Regardless of the reason, they are left to die alone, often with hospital, nursing home or hospice staff as the only ones around who care.

True love and concern can exist from health care professionals for their patients. But it can almost never be the same as the love and caring that are part of lifelong relationships. That is the kind of concern most people long for, and it is dread of not having it that makes people afraid of getting old. Aging in and of itself is not the problem. It's being old and ill and *alone* that is frightening.

How can you be a friend to your "single" friend who is dying and who has no (involved) family around him?

The suggestions for listening, talking, doing, and touching given in the preceding section can all be used in this situation.

But there are things unique to the situation of trying to be a friend to a person dying without (close) relatives that should be considered.

Primarily, know that *no matter what*, you alone cannot be all things to your friend that he may want or need you to be during his dying process. To repeat: *No matter what*, you alone cannot be all things to your friend.

At the time of initial diagnosis, your single friend may say that until his illness is unavoidably noticeable, you are the only person he is going to tell that he is terminally ill. This is an unfair burden to put on you—and on himself. The desire of some terminally ill people to retain the routines of their daily living as long as possible is normal. But the burden of silent knowing is too much for both of you, as well as for your ongoing friendship.

Tell your friend that you care a great deal about him and you hope his dying will not happen for a very long time. But that when he is nearer death, you want to be able to be there for him as much as possible. If you and he are the only ones who know his situation for much of this preferably long time, the burden may become too great for you, and you may be less able to "be there" throughout than you would want.

Then sit down with your friend and together think of some other people who could be told—perhaps people with different kinds of relationships with your friend than you have. Offer to tell these people yourself, with your friend's permission, if he doesn't feel up to it.

At other times, when a person is initially told he has a terminal illness, he will tell everyone immediately. This can be a way for the person to deal with his shock, a way to try to make his "terminal" diagnosis seem real. But telling everyone immediately about a terminal diagnosis can have its drawbacks, too.

As mentioned earlier, some people will be so devastated by this sudden turn of events in their friend's life that they will begin to see him as already dead. This is "part one" of the vulture syndrome, in which people gather only at the person's "coming-out" (news of a terminal diagnosis) and "going-out" (final stages of dying).

Too many people gathered together too soon, *with no one having any clearly defined sense of purpose, can be counterproductive.* Many of these people will be overwhelmed by the crowd and by the sense of urgency resulting from all the "news bulletins." As a defense against their own feelings of impotence and pain, they may prematurely bury their friend, in order not to have to suffer with him during the course of his dying. And then they won't be around to help when they are needed.

When "family"—relatives—are involved, these situations are more carefully controlled. They see to it that the news filters out gradually, and that friends visit only in small groups, as invited or requested. But in the absence of family, often no one person or core group oversees the situation, and the result can be chaos.

If your single friend confides in you when he receives a terminal diagnosis, you can be his friend by encouraging him to tell others as well—but not everyone at once—and by helping him limit the number of people who initially gather and who give out information.

When a terminally ill person has no (close) relatives, definition of helper roles can be difficult. Some people want to do everything, to take over when they are not necessarily wanted in that role by the dying person. Other people always assume someone else already is doing whatever they may think to do. And still others are too much in shock to take any initiative. At times people who were not previously close to a person who is dying end up doing much more than expected, because the people who are close to him are so far gone in preliminary mourning that they cannot perform effectively as comforters.

Assuming your friend who is dying has a number of friends still living, someone will begin to emerge as his choice for closest confidant. This same person is also likely to emerge as the unofficial spokesperson, and increasingly the intermediary, in matters surrounding your friend's dying. If this person is not you and if you feel it should have been, *never* is the time to say something about those feelings. Perhaps your dying friend didn't want to burden you with so much pain *because* of your closeness, and he is protecting your friendship for moments together that really count to you both. Or, perhaps he just feels more comfortable dying with his other friend ''in control.'' We're not always closest in our day-to-day living with our ''take-charge'' friends. But they may become the friends we're closest to in our day-to-day dying.

If you do emerge as your dying single friend's closest confidant and intermediary, *be very sure you want and can take on this role*. Your friend needs someone in this role. If you feel you can't do it, sleep on it two nights, and then if you feel the same way, tell your friend you can't.

Sometimes fear takes hold of us when we think we're a key person in living out someone's dying with him. If it's fear alone that is bothering you, you're normal. It is scary. Sleep on it two nights and you'll probably realize you can do the impossible just as well as anyone else.

But if it is more than fear, tell your friend up front. It is better to be honest with him at the start than leave him wondering why you seem increasingly distant or less available as time goes on and his situation worsens.

If he says that you are the only person whom he feels close

enough to turn to as confidant and intermediary during his dying, but you don't feel comfortable in that role, tell him so as gently as possible. Tell him you want to be sure there will be sufficient support for him throughout, so you would like to contact a hospice, church group and/or a community home help agency *in the beginning* so that additional support will be available as needed over time. Gathering such support early on makes it easier for your friend, for you, and for all concerned by establishing a pattern of familiar care that can be supportive throughout. (Requesting early support from such trained groups or agencies *is often wise* regardless of the number of friends or family available.)

If you do take on the role of closest support and confidant to your terminally ill single friend, remember that first rule of thumb: *No matter what*, you alone cannot be all things to your friend that he may want or need you to be during his dying process.

The second rule is: No one knows how much time will be involved between the terminal diagnosis and the death. So, don't try to outguess or outrun death. You must pace yourself for the long haul—even if it sounds like very little time.

Your friend's physician may have given him a "ball-park" timeframe for life expectancy. *But it's only a guess.* Most physicians *hate* to give time estimates where death is involved. Understandably, however, most people who are terminally ill want to know how long they might expect to live. And if a terminally ill person wants to know this he has a right, I feel, to be given the physician's *best guess*. Everyone involved must then remember that it *is* only a guess.

No matter how short a time between the diagnosis and the death, if you approach your friend's dying with "overkill" of love and attention from the beginning, you may wear yourself out before he dies, and cease to be able to help. This can be devastating to both of you.

Be as close as you can be to your terminally ill friend *while still maintaining your own life apart from the dying process*. This is very important, and very difficult. You can get so involved in the dying of a friend (or family member) that the rest of your world ceases to provide any meaningful involvement. This is not totally wrong, but it can present problems, especially in the case of a "friend" trying to be the primary support to a dying friend.

With family members, public sanction is given to be intensely involved and to mourn, both before and after the person's death. But if you are not a relative, if you are "only a friend," even though you may be the primary source of support, tenderness, and love to your dying friend, you will be given little, if any, public sanction for your role. You will have to bear your emotional and practical burdens alone, in all likelihood.

The comments earlier in this book on friend as mourner are unfortunately just as applicable to friend as primary support to a dying friend. Somehow we seem to expect single people who are dying to die without anyone around them who cares as much as family would. We seem willing to give only blood relatives the right to make sacrifices of love and to mourn that love when it is gone, despite the fact that at times a single person may have a family of friends closer than his natural family.

So, your role as primary support to your dying single friend may be lonely from the view of public acceptance and credibility.

If your dying friend has many other friends, your role as primary support may also meet with resentment from some who wanted to fill the role themselves or who want to be more involved; or with benign apathy from some who are in shock or who feel all your dying friend's needs are being met by you. *It is important to involve these people in one way or another, as much as possible, from the beginning.* You may need to exercise the skills of a peacemaker and of a camp activities counselor to do so; but developing and using the involvement and skills of other friends *in the beginning* will help in untold ways down the road—especially if that road is a long one.

Don't give in to the temptations of martyrdom. You may dearly love your friend and not feel martyred at all by being with her as much as you can in her dying. But nonetheless, as her primary support, it is inevitable that you are giving up other things in your daily life and enduring added pressures in order to be part of a unique sharing. So deep inside you are feeling good about you; and seeing a certain beauty in the falling away of most of the facades and trivias that are part of our daily lives. You are coming into contact with raw edges of feelings and strengths within yourself that you may never before have touched. This is good—but it can be dangerous too.

You may try to do too much. You feel special because it is you your friend has "chosen" to live out her dying with her; you she has asked to share her precious last months on earth. This often subconscious sense of being "special" can impede your initiative to involve those whom shock or benign apathy has kept at a distance, those whom your friend has not turned to as primary caretakers. Be on guard for this.

Those who were asked only for limited involvement *do care* nonetheless. Try to include them in some way—perhaps by asking them to keep other friends informed of the sick person's condition, or by grocery shopping, or helping with transportation needs, or forming a prayer circle. There are many ways people who care can help.

Those fearful of involvement need to talk out their fears and be offered supportive presence in any visits; and those who think they aren't needed need to be assured that their help, too, is welcome.

Friends also can be reminded how much an occasional— perhaps even weekly—card saying "hi" can mean to someone ill. Sending cards is simple and maintains ongoing caring contact.

If you find yourself feeling a sense of "specialness" as a result of your role as primary support in your friend's dying, be cautious, especially if this is leading you to exclude other concerned friends. Remember, *no matter what*, you cannot be all things to your friend that she will want or need during her dying process. And if you take on all the responsibility, you may "burn out" before she dies, leaving her with no one else who feels more than remotely needed or comfortable to step in and help.

Another danger of allowing your friend to depend too exclusively on you is that she will also focus her anger—anger in reality related to her approaching death—on you. She may accuse you of not "being there" enough for her. This can happen even if you have been bending over backwards to be involved and to care.

Your friend's reaction is normal. A person can become very self-oriented when the future of that "self" is limited and when she sees everyone around her having seemingly limitless futures in comparison. "You're healthy; you have years ahead of you," she may say. "Why can't you spend a few measly days with me?'' But this is all the more reason to encourage other friends to become involved in one way or another in your friend's dying process. Their participation can give her enough support that her anger can be defused or, at least, diffused among a greater number.

Sometimes, however, anger can be neither defused nor diffused, neither smoothed over nor simply allowed to be expressed without rebuttal. The anger is very real, and usually comes from fear of being alone and frustration with the pain and difficulty of the dying process—not from anything you have done. Both you and your friend must remember that. And it may become necessary for you to remind her.

If you never confront your friend's anger toward you, you will soon become an easy mark for misdirected anger, which could lead to a cooling off of your friendship before your friend's death. This can leave her even more alone, and could leave you with unfounded but nonetheless very real guilt feelings.

One area in which you may wish to involve other friends is that of legal and financial planning. Your dying friend may ask you to help with her affairs before and after her death. If you have a head for this and know what it entails, and if you feel comfortable doing so, by all means agree. It will take a weight off her mind. *But be very sure you know exactly what is entailed.* It may require more involvement, especially after the death and funeral, than you may envision and, therefore, *could hinder the normal completion of your mourning process.*

You may be wise to ask your friend to seek preliminary legal and/or financial counsel to determine exactly what will be involved. It will be difficult to decide to say no to a request to handle affairs when your friend is still alive. But it may prove even harder to carry out her request after she has died.

You may want to find out whether your state provides some way in which you can share involvement in settling her affairs, either with another friend or with a professional. This sharing offers you backup support if the ongoing legalities become harmful to your healing process after your friend's death. She would rather you be frank with her now than saddle yourself with something that becomes a burden to you after her death.

Your friend's illness may often take her to the hospital. Or, she may spend most or all of her illness at home. Either way— though particularly if she is at home—your friend may require some form of physical care that you could assist with. *Do not try to do all of this yourself.* It may be possible for you to do it all, but at most times it is unwise.

Learning certain care techniques can be of help and comfort to you both. Emptying a urine collection bag, for example, is simple. Giving an occasional injection, with some instruction and practice (on an orange—not on your friend!) is not hard.

But trying to perform all of an ill friend's care, especially as that care becomes more complicated or frequent, can put pressure on the relationship and not leave time or energy for you to share the most important thing—the friendship itself.

There are a variety of home health agencies and hospice services in most communities now. This is another reason to urge your friend to contact one early on so their personnel and services can become familiar and unthreatening.

As mentioned earlier, never promise someone you will be with her at the moment of death unless you are *absolutely certain* you can be. Chances are great she won't know who is with her when she dies. But if you are not there, your potential feelings of guilt could grow out of proportion to all the good you've done along the way.

Actions are better than promises anyway. Doing what you can as you can will say much more than making lots of promises you are in danger of not keeping.

If you have been a friend in any capacity to your single friend during his or her dying, know that you have done a good thing. Know, too, that you have a *right to mourn*; and *claim* that right to mourn. Don't be embarrassed or afraid to say you are mourning your friend's death. This advice is particularly necessary for you to remember if you were deeply involved in your friend's dying.

Because you were friend and not "family" to your dying friend, you probably received no public sanction or acceptance for your role in her dying, or your feelings of mourning for her death. Things around you have probably gone on *at exactly the same pace as they would have* had you not been involved in your friend's dying, even if you were her primary support. Most people around you have expected you to perform "as usual" during the whole process, giving little if any leeway for your mourning.

So one day—still in a state of unacknowledged, unsanctioned mourning—you wake up and find that your friend has died and you are feeling that nothing in your life is worthwhile; not your family and friends, not your job, not your living situation . . . perhaps not even yourself. You think, "If my friend could die, then I also could die . . . and if this is all there is to my life now, I'd better get busy and make changes; I'd better start stuffing my life full of new meaning and new challenges."

This is the time you may react by wanting to move, change jobs, and/or give up old friends for new. Though revitalizing our lives isn't a bad thing to do in any circumstance, the "one-year rule" is still a good one to follow, whether it's a close friend or a family member whom you have lost. Your home, your job, your town, and your ordinary "less-special" friends may take on new luster if you wait one year after your friend's death before making any major changes in your life. In one year your mourning probably will be worked through in great measure. And the compounded pressures that were piled on you when you were expected to function normally while mourning your friend's dying and death will have been eased.

Meanwhile you must expect to feel surprisingly intense emotions of loss and self-questioning (which may emerge for a time as self-depreciation and feeling out of sync with everyone and everything around you) *because you are mourning.* The friend you loved and cared about died, and you were directly involved in sharing that process with her.

No one may ever tell you that you are feeling as you do because you are mourning. Or, if someone does tell you, you may not hear him because he may be the only one; or because you may feel your mourning as "friend" should be limited or submerged. This is nonsense. You loved your friend. When we lose someone or something we love we have a *right* to mourn. And, regardless, we *will* mourn. So it is far better to claim that right than to deny it and suffer the additional pain of thwarted or incomplete mourning.

After all, your friend is *worth* being mourned, is she not?

7

When the Loss Isn't Death

THE TROUBLE WITH trying to mourn loss when death isn't involved is that there is no body, no funeral, and no public shoulder to cry on. There is no traditional, socially sanctioned outlet for mourning when the loss isn't death.

Loss of function, relationship, or financial resources, for example, bring no printed obituary, no "remains" laid to rest, no public gathering to cement the fact and focus love on the mourner.

Trying to mourn loss when death is not involved is a lonely hell, with vague beginnings and endings defined more often by the intangible dimensions of lost and found hope than by the perimeters of the crisis itself.

As example, a person is rendered permanently paralyzed from the neck down immediately upon impact in an auto accident. But that person does not fully mourn his loss until he acknowledges not just the paralysis, but its permanence. And he cannot begin to heal—to have renewed belief in self and in life—until he mourns his loss in all its fullness.

Divorce papers may be signed, separate homes may exist, custody rights may be resolved; but if either person has an unrealistic hope of reconciliation, his or her mourning process cannot tip the balance from hurt toward healing.

Severance pay may be in the bank and office keys turned in;

but if a person still waits by the phone for a never-to-come callback to his lost job, false hope is inhibiting his mourning.

How then can one be a friend to someone mourning tragedies such as these? Do we hit him over the head with a baseball bat and say, "Get on with it, fellow. There's no hope here. Accept your loss and weep." Or do we say: "Every cloud has a silver lining." "There's a light at the end of the tunnel." "God never closes a door but that He opens a window." "Just pick yourself up by your bootstraps and go on!" "Tomorrow is another day!" "You'll be a better person for it all."

Well, if you're like me you probably have said one or more of those things to a friend in crisis. And, like me, you may have wished you hadn't!

To be a friend to someone mourning loss other than death it is important to remember and accept that your friend *is* mourning. In fact, in some instances losses not involving death *may* be more deeply felt. A divorce may cause greater pain than the peaceful death of one's eighty-six-year-old granddad. Permanent paralysis may bring as much or more suffering than the death of a cold and distant parent. Loss of a dream or a beloved job may cause as much grief as the death of a severely retarded child.

To be a friend to someone mourning a loss other than death it is important to remember and accept that your friend's mourning is deep and real. Just as we are often guilty of "rushing" people through mourning for death, so are we even more often guilty of rushing our friends through mourning other losses—*if* we allow them to mourn at all.

A person mourning a tragic non-death loss needs time to mourn and affirmation that it is acceptable and normal to mourn, just as does the person mourning a death.

This normal mourning process includes shock, hurt, and healing, and proceeds in a fashion generally comparable to the death mourning process described earlier. It also can be helped in great measure by listening, talking, doing, and touching, as described in Chapter Six.

However, let's look more closely at disability, divorce, and career setbacks—three major non-death losses—for any particular or additional things friends can do to help in such circumstances.

DISABILITY

There are many types of disabilities. I choose to use as example sudden-onset, complete quadriplegia—permanent paralysis reaching from the chest on down. But many of the following suggestions could apply in dealing with a number of other disabilities.

Before I went to work as chaplain at The Rehabilitation Institute of Chicago, I figured that working with dying children and their families was the hardest hospital ministry I could do. I was wrong. "Rehab," for me, was harder.

A rehabilitation hospital such as R.I.C. treats people with severe physical disabilities and, increasingly now, people with severe brain trauma. An acute care hospital may also have a rehabilitation unit, but usually it isn't equipped or staffed for the complicated problems handled by a major rehabilitation hospital such as R.I.C. R.I.C. is a tertiary care rehab hospital, a "Rolls-Royce" of rehabilitation medicine, if you will.

All that would look nice on a resumé, if I were looking for another job. But day to day it means R.I.C. cares for lots of people who are suffering some of the most traumatic disabilities known. And governmental economic policies notwithstanding, a great number of these people *must* stay at Rehab for several months—long enough for staff to get to know them far beyond the diagnosis, to get to know them as people.

Such closeness can also occur in work with children or adults who are dying. But there is a key difference: with death comes an end. With major, permanent physical disability comes a cloud that never completely lifts. This cloud can lighten; it can become routine; it can be forgotten or ignored for increasingly longer periods of time. But it never completely disappears. The disabled body part(s) is an ever-present reminder of the loss.

And so, in the long run, over the long haul, I have found it emotionally more difficult to minister to people with severe physical disabilities than to children who are dying and their families.

This same difficulty I found in ministry may hold true with friendship. It *may* be harder, for some people, to be a friend to someone with a disability than to someone mourning a loss involving death. Both friend and chaplain may find death's finality easier to deal with than a disability's permanence.

There are two key things to remember as you begin trying to be a friend to someone mourning a sudden-onset permanent disability:

1. *Initially*, especially if you have seen him in the hospital, it will be easier for you than for your friend to believe in the fact of his disability. (This usually is true unless you had something to do with the reason he is disabled. Then your guilt likely will block any initial belief that your friend is disabled.)

2. It will become harder for both you and your friend to proceed through the process of mourning his disability as you realize that the evidence of that disability continues to remain with him, often in plain sight, every hour of every day of every week. . . . (In some ways, it is as if the parent of a dead child were forced to carry that child's body around with him wherever he went for the rest of his life—a constant, ever-present reminder of his loss.)

Therefore, to be a friend to someone with a sudden onset physical disability it is important to realize: He may have a different degree of hope for his situation than you do at any given time, especially in the beginning. And the actual mourning process may be far longer and harder for both of you than either of you may expect.

To be a friend to someone with a physical disability it is important not just to remember these things, but to *do* one other thing: You and your friend have to see each other with enough frequency that the primary focus of your shared relationship can move *beyond* the disability without totally annihilating that disability from any future discussion.

The person with sudden-onset disability who has a normal mourning process experiences shock, hurt, and healing, always intermingled with hope in its many forms. It is important for you, as his friend, to listen to *and share* his hope without engendering false hope.

When I was new at Rehab—the first full-time chaplain they ever had—the only referrals I would receive from physicians came when their patients talked of a miracle cure. "You'd better see Joe Jones. He says God's going to heal him on Easter."

To have hope for a miracle cure or healing when one is suddenly paralyzed for life is a *normal* shock reaction. It is a defense not only against believing that something that horrible could happen to you, but that it will be with you for the rest of your life.

Hope for a miracle cure or healing doesn't come only with shock, however. In many cases it returns, off and on in one form or another, for the rest of a disabled person's life. At any time when reality of life with the disability becomes *too* real for *too* long, a person can hope for a miraculous cure—though he may admit this to others less and less frequently the further post-injury he gets. *This occasional hope for a miraculous cure is not abnormal, even if it is unrealistic.*

It is only when hope for miraculous deliverance or swift cure inhibits daily efforts to live life as it now exists that a problem can arise.

To be a friend to someone with a disability who tells you he hopes for a "miraculous cure," it is all right to hope with him—as long as that hope is not fed in such a way that it keeps him from doing what he can do, and being who he can be, in the absence of a miracle. "I hope you are cured (or healed) too, Joe. But you're my friend regardless. And it's important to keep your body as strong as possible each day while we wait and hope."

If the cure happens as Joe wants, great! If it doesn't, he'll be the first to know. And you will have helped him live more fully in the meantime.

A more common and usually longer lasting form of hope that is normal for someone with a sudden-onset disability is the hope that if he works hard enough at his therapies, or is good enough, or both, he will "get his strength back again." This is, in one way or another, a form of bargaining. And at times in our lives bargaining with ourselves pays off. (Bargaining with God doesn't work—but, then, this isn't the God chapter). It certainly won't hurt to work hard or try to "be good." But it may not help in exactly the way your friend is hoping, either.

The best thing you can do for your friend during this time is to support him in his endeavors, but at the same time, as before, *support him for who he is today*. "I hope you can walk again someday too, Joe. But just remember you're my friend whether you're walking or not. You'll always be my friend. You aren't less a person because of this, you know."

If your friend does get his "strength back," great! If he

doesn't, you will have helped him begin to believe in himself as worthwhile regardless of whether he can walk.

These or other forms of hope may come not only during initial shock, but may recur with any physical improvement your friend may make over the years, with any medical advances in relevant areas, or, again, at times when the reality of living with his disability simply becomes too overwhelming.

In time, however, the hope of a person with a disability becomes more than hope for return of normal function. It is hope in its purest form.

A few years back I was asked to write an article for the *Christian Century* on ministry to people with physical disabilities.

In the article ("Save Your Roof! Build a Ramp!" Dec. 12, 1979, pp. 1237–1241) I discussed this very real form of hope:

A recent popular Broadway play called *Whose Life is It Anyway?* is about a sculptor who became quadriplegic in an accident, and about his battle to have his life-sustaining catheter removed so that he can die. The play does make a point about self-determination. But its story line is not what generally happens in real life, surprising as that was to me for a long time. It's not what really happens with the many people I know who are quadriplegic. These people do go on living—actually *fight* to go on living.

And for what? I asked myself this question for a long time. What makes life worth living for a quadriplegic person? Despite acute-care and rehab hospitalization, despite some improvement and learned skills, this person still cannot dress independently, eat without help, completely control bodily functions or have sex in any of the 101 ways (though there are ways). And likely the person cannot maneuver into his or her own parish church anymore.

Wouldn't someone in this situation really be better off dead? Why more often than not does the person who is quadriplegic fight to go on living?

Such a person fights, I believe, not because death is more fearsome than this type of life, but because he or she still has *hope*. Hope to walk again? Yes. Despite the odds, no quadriplegic person I know has ever totally given up hope of someday walking again. Hope for a medical breakthrough, hope for an "act of God"—hope somewhere deep down inside, hope that does not quit.

But the hope that makes a person who is quadriplegic go on living—*fight* to go on living—is more than hope to walk again one day. More so, it is hope in life, hope that sometime—today, tomorrow, next year—life will be better. Many people who are quadriplegic work hard to make that hope come true. They work hard to add breadth and dimension to their lives, to grow and to learn, to give and to experience. In that, they are like you and me. For all persons, hope is the food of our tomorrows, the "anchor of the soul," and when we lose hope, we lose life—whether we are disabled or not.

And so there is a danger when those of us who are not quadriplegic assume that those who are would be better off dead: we may rob someone of that intangible human quality of hope which does not die when one's spinal cord is severed. Hope dies only when one's tomorrows are cut off. And that can happen to *anyone*.

You can be a friend to your friend with a disability by sharing with him your faith in him—and in the value of life. This means helping him live to the fullest each day while not denying him the right to hope for a cure; helping him work hard to "regain strength," while affirming him as a total, worthwhile human being in the midst of his struggle; and by being his friend for the duration, thus affirming one of the most important reasons to live that any of us can have: the love of true friendship.

Hope, both realistic and unrealistic, is part of your friend's active mourning process and beyond. But hope is not the only component of your friend's mourning process.

Your friend with sudden-onset permanent disability will experience great emotional *pain*, as does the person mourning death, once he allows himself to believe that his disability is permanent. But the time he begins this, the time he enters the pain phase of mourning, may be far down the road from the date of onset of his disability. The shock and the pain involved in mourning the permanency of a sudden-onset disability can play leapfrog with each other for a long time before the pain phase of mourning takes the commanding lead. You well may think your friend is "coming along fine" two to three months after his injury when, in fact, the reality of permanent disability is just beginning to hit him, and the pain of his true mourning is just starting.

In this world most adults have had enough experience with death to know intellectually that it is permanent. Most adults have experienced the death of someone they love.

But in this world, most people have *not* personally experienced that a disability such as paralysis can be permanent. Paralysis or other disabilities are just not in most people's "ball park" of daily living.

So it will probably take your friend far longer than you may expect to even *begin* the pain of mourning his loss. (In fact, a few people *never* move through the process of pain in mourning their disabilities. They jump, instead, from shock to an incomplete form of emotional healing. This is too complicated to go into here. Suffice it to say that this process has some similarities to the traditional male trying to mourn his dead loved one by jumping from shock to healing. (See Chapter Five.)

How long this painful phase of mourning lasts can depend on a huge number of variables—far more variables than are usually involved in the pain of mourning death. A great number of these variables have to do with the inner and outer resources your friend had *before* the onset of his disability. There is a sad saying that floats around rehab hospitals, "If you're going to be a quad, get a degree and a desk job first."

So often people who are suddenly disabled are involved in manual labor jobs or are so young they haven't finished or even started their higher education.

Having a completed education and a desk job may be a help to your friend in adjusting to his disability. But so will having family and friends, like you, who maintain contact with him and quietly but convincingly reinforce him as a worthwhile person— worthy of love and friendship regardless of any disability.

It can help to begin to focus on his assets. *But not to the exclusion of his valid need to mourn his gigantic loss and experience the pain that will come with the growing reality of permanence.*

Often at the beginning of mourning sudden-onset disability, the *fear of being trapped* is so overpowering it is almost all-consuming for a time. And unfortunately it is often at about this same time, in the beginning of this consuming fear and pain of mourning, that a person will be near discharge from the rehabilitation hospital and will have to make some major decisions for his immediate future.

Fear of being trapped in a disabled body or mind and facing inadequate financial resources, living arrangements, health care, safety, vocational opportunity, and social life are just some of the goblins that, along with anger, guilt, and hopelessness, may haunt your friend as he tries to juggle his anguish and his need to make concrete decisions for his future.

If you can offer real, tangible help in any of these areas, do so. Relieving even the smallest pressure for even the shortest time can be of great help. But be sure you are actually able to fulfill any commitments you make. And if you have more than passing doubts, don't make the commitment at all. Your friend is feeling rejected enough ''by life'' as it is.

What about you in all of this so far? Surprising though it may be, it is when your friend is discharged from the hospital that you may discover *you are progressing at a slower rate in your mourning of his loss than he is*!

Seeing your friend after his discharge from a rehabilitation hospital may be the turning point in your coming to believe in the reality of his disability. Until now you likely have seen your friend only in the hospital setting or on a weekend home visit from which he will return to the hospital. As hospital patients, people are ''supposed'' to be sick, to have something wrong with them, to look different. It is not as difficult to believe someone is paralyzed when we see him hospitalized in a wheelchair with limp limbs.

But when the person comes home, he is no longer a hospital patient. He may be weak for a while; but he is ''supposed'' to be better, to be healed.

Your friend has lived for maybe several months now as a person unable to move certain parts of his body. That reality of immobility likely is beginning to set in in earnest for him.

But you may only have seen him a few times, always still as a hospital patient. The pain of beginning to believe, not that your friend is paralyzed, but that that paralysis is *permanent* may come for the first time only when you see your friend at home and he still can't walk; he's still sitting in a wheelchair.

The two of you can't ''run'' out for a hamburger. You can't play tennis together. You can't hop a bus to the movies. It slowly dawns on you that a certain kind of previously taken-for-granted *spontaneity* in your friendship is virtually gone. And for you, the pain of mourning your friend's loss—and deep inside, mourning what you begin to fear may be your own loss of a friendship—begins in earnest. Not only will things never quite be the same again; things won't be even close to the same again.

But such thoughts are scary and certainly disloyal, you quickly realize. So you put them away. Your friend is a good friend. You won't let him down! You'll be there!

And you are there. But how you are there and how you handle your feelings in these next months can be vital if you truly want to try to "be there" in a continuing, sharing friendship for the duration.

Earlier I said there were two things to remember and one thing to do in trying to be a friend to a person with a physical disability. The thing to do was to be with your friend, communicate with your friend, "with enough frequency that the primary focus of your shared relationship can move beyond the disability, without totally annihilating that disability from any future discussion."

With enough frequency: Those are the words that can be the key now.

The typical mistake people make in trying to be a friend to someone just home from the hospital with a newly acquired permanent disability is to smother him with attention. *Most of the time, this is a misjudgment.*

Your friend needs time and space to adjust to his new situation. And *you* do, too.

In the chapter on dying, I mentioned the "vulture syndrome," in which people converge on a person at his "coming-out"—when news of his terminal illness is public, and his "going-out"—his dying.

Well, your friend isn't dying. (In fact, he's probably in excellent physical health apart from his disability.) But his coming home is his "coming-out" in a sense. It is the first time many people may have felt reasonably comfortable—and safe—in visiting, knowing that family members and other friends would likely be there.

So the house is filled with well-wishers in person and on the phone. For a while. Then the house may be filled with silence.

To be a friend to a friend recently returned to his community with a disability, *take your time and give him his time without ever losing all contact or continuity*. And know that this can be a difficult time for you both.

Many well-meaning people smother their new disabled friend with kindness upon kindness in the beginning—until the time that they begin to believe his disability is permanent. Then the painful reality sets in, and they become aware of the logistical and emotional barriers to being friends with a person with a permanent disability, especially a disability necessitating the use of "devices" such as wheelchairs, sign language, or braille.

Being a sharing friend with Joe slowly but surely comes to seem like too much work. For a while, going to his home and "hanging around" with him seems OK. But then guilt—and maybe resentment—creep in that that is all you ever do with Joe any more; when "before" you went bowling and fishing together as well. Soon visits with Joe become less and less frequent . . . or stop altogether.

If you truly want to be active friends with your friend for the duration of his disability—which may be the duration of his life—start slowly *but steadily*. Visit occasionally, and telephone in between, or send cards or letters. Ask yourself how often you saw or talked with Joe before his injury. If it was a great deal, you may not feel able to do as much right now. *And neither may he!* But a card or phone calls between visits still say you care.

It may be more difficult now to do "outside" things with your friend. But it may not be as difficult as you and even he imagine, especially after you've done them a time or two.

Assuming your friend has had good rehabilitation he will know what he needs when he goes out. All you have to do is: (1) want him to be part of your excursion and let him know that, and (2) *ask him* to tell you what you need to do to make this possible. Some things he can take care of on his own. Others, perhaps like getting his wheelchair up and down some steps, may require help.

In the beginning certain outings will require some advance thought and planning. *But the more you do it the easier it gets*. Soon it is a matter of routine.

And with the return of a form of routine can come the return of spontaneity. One day you'll realize you *don't even see* your friend's wheelchair or guide dog or braces any more. And that will give you a tremendous boost. You'll know you and your friend can enjoy things together again; and that though things may not be "the same" again, they are *OK*! They are moving on.

But haven't I left something out of this section? What do you *SAY*? All these months of shock and pain and healing that have gone on. What do you say?

The same advice as was given in the mourning chapter holds true. If you are a listening friend, listen for the anger, the guilt, the questioning of God and the other emotions that are part of the mourning process. Affirm that what happened to your friend is awful. Affirm his hope. Affirm his worth. Don't be judgmental. And do keep lines of communication open even when he doesn't want to talk.

Say he's still your friend by touching him now and again. Sometimes, especially in the pain of mourning, people with disabilities feel ugly or untouchable. No one wants to feel this way. Let your friend know he's still "touchable" by touching him in a normal manner. If his disability includes something contagious, observe medical precautions, of course. But you can still touch even if it is through sterile gloves.

What about using words like "running" or "dashing" or "walking," "seeing" or "looking," or "hearing" or "listening"—if your friend can't do those things?

Each person is different. But in a number of cases, these words *may sting a lot in the early stages of mourning*—when the person is just beginning to believe the disability is permanent. Although I know that not using such words won't make the paralysis, blindness, or deafness go away, I personally am cautious about using them with someone *in the pain stage of mourning disability*. And I am even more cautious about using them as part of a complaint—about "having to walk to work in the cold and snow," for example, or "having to read reports 'til the wee hours," or "having to listen to boring speech after boring speech."

Yes, I know my words don't add to the person's disability or make it permanent. But with a fresh wound, if you can avoid rubbing salt in it for a little while until a scab forms it can be a kindness.

I'm sure some other rehab professionals would disagree, as would most people who have been disabled for a while and take such phrases and comments "in stride." But I work where the wounds are fresh, and the feelings are more raw than some can or wish to remember. So, I will continue to try to use some caution in phrasing when talking with a person in the pain of mourning his disability.

Some clues to when a person may be in this painful phase of mourning are: a certain amount of withdrawal; less enthusiasm for working hard; less talk of hope; displays of anger, hurt, guilt, and/or hopelessness; and physical symptoms not previously evident.

As the hurt of mourning wanes and healing begins, your friend will be increasingly prepared to tackle day-to-day living beyond his disability. As this happens, it becomes even more important for you to remember that Joe is your "friend, Joe." He is only *secondarily* your friend who has a disability.

Joe should be just "Joe." *Work at it.* Joe. Period. Not "my disabled friend," or "the handicapped guy," or "the guy in the chair." Just Joe. It gets easier. And it reminds both you and others that Joe's wheelchair (or guide dog or sign language) is only a means to an end—mobility—and not a part of who Joe is.

If ever it is necessary to mention that Joe is in a wheelchair for logistical reasons, that's OK. But try to teach yourself not to think of or discuss your friend always in terms of his disability.

A person with a disability is a person first. The more you can think of your friend and relate to him as a total person, the more you can share in his—and others—learning to see himself in that way. And that is sharing in your friend's healing and in your learning.

A common mistake people make in seeing someone with one disability is to treat him as if he is *totally* disabled—so totally disabled that he almost doesn't exist. This often happens in restaurants, for example, where a waiter—referring to a person in a wheelchair—will ask his able-bodied friend, "What will he have?" as though he not only can't walk, but also can't hear or talk or think.

Remember and help others learn that people in wheelchairs can usually do all the things that other people can do—except walk; and that, in general, a person with one disability rarely has multiple sensory disabilities or retardation.

Other things to remember are that a wheelchair is part of its owner's personal space. It is not there to be leaned on or to hang things from. Also, an adult or teen in a wheelchair *hates* to be patted on the head or treated in any other way as less mature than his years.

A person in a wheelchair would also greatly appreciate it if you would sit down near him if the two of you are going to converse in more than passing greeting. Constantly having to talk with one's neck crooked upward can be painful.

If your friend decides to transfer from his wheelchair to a standard seat, don't move the wheelchair out of his reach without his permission and knowledge of its new location.

If blindness is your friend's disability, let him know who and where you are as you approach him. And if there are others present and you are addressing him directly, make sure he knows that.

If your friend has a guide dog, don't assume the dog can be petted. Most people with guide dogs treat them as the trained professionals they are and allow few people, if any, to pet or play with them when they are working. The simple rule of thumb is, don't pet a guide dog or otherwise play with or distract him.

Know, too, that your friend's guide dog usually is very special to him. If the dog dies or must be put to sleep, this can cause your friend great trauma. Be sympathetic almost as you would had your friend lost a human friend.

Don't assume a person who is blind reads braille or has better-developed "other senses." Some do; but don't assume.

If you're on an outing with a person who is blind, you might describe the scenery to him if he wishes. Ask. Even people blind from birth can enjoy this.

When walking with a blind friend who is without cane or guide dog, let him take your arm and walk slightly behind you. This can give him a sense of security.

Your friend may be legally blind but still have some sense of sight. This doesn't mean he has 20-20 vision, and it's important for you not to forget this! If you have a question as to whether or not he can see something relevant, ask him. Don't assume.

If a deaf person lost his hearing relatively late in life, it may be difficult or impossible at times for those who don't know him to realize he is deaf. If, however, he has never heard language or has forgotten sounds, his speech may sound very different, and people who don't know him may think he is retarded. Don't assume someone who talks differently is retarded. Find out if he has a hearing problem and then ask him how you can best communicate with him.

If he has a hearing aid, don't shout, but do speak clearly, in close proximity, facing him. He may be reading your lips, too; though this alone won't tell him every word you're saying. Be willing to repeat anything he may not have understood.

If you can learn sign language, great. Be sure it's the same one (there are several) your friend knows. But don't assume all deaf people know sign language. Some choose other ways to communicate. Ask the person. Be willing to write things out until the two of you can come up with a better system.

And finally, what about helping your friend, or anyone with a disability, who appears to be in a problematic or dangerous situation? *Ask the person himself if he would like help.* (Unless, of course, it is a danger that is immediate, such as a car about to run down a blind person. Then act first and ask later!) If he says yes, ask him to direct you how best to help him.

There are volumes of funny and far-from-funny stories among people with disabilities about well-meaning people who saw them in what appeared to be problematic situations and "helped" them into situations they'd rather not have been in.

Unless there is imminent and real danger, ask the person himself if he needs help. If he does want some help, ask him to direct you how best to help him.

One day the time comes when you can talk with your friend about you again. You are over the biggest hurdles of mourning— both your friend's mourning and your mourning.

You have taken your time and given him his time and consistently kept the windows of communication between you open.

You have braved the logistics of doing things "outside the house" often enough that you've learned the tricks and established a routine.

You've been careful, during the days when the pain of his loss was still raw, not to dwell on words or situations that might have exacerbated that pain.

You've asked him to tell you how best you could help him.

All in all, you've been a friend. And now the time of reciprocity has returned. *Now you can and should let your friend care once again about what is happening to you.* He is ready,

willing and able, and may well have a sensitivity and understanding that you'll find in few others.

MOURNING DISCOVERY OF DISABILITY IN A CHILD

Discovering one's child or grandchild has been born with a
disability is a terrible sorrow, for children are our link with
immortality. The mourning done at this time is for all the lost
hopes and dreams that the child can never realize because of his
disability. But it is important to remember that this loss of hope
need not be total, though that is how it may seem in the beginning.

If your friend gives birth to a disabled child, she will feel with
great intensity all the emotions of mourning. It may be difficult
for your friend to admit that she and her husband are mourning
because the infant is alive and, in its innocence, is waiting and
wanting to be loved, and they will feel guilty about mourning.
But mourning is normal and necessary for parents and grandparents, and does not mean that they do not love the child.

There are of course situations where parents of a disabled
child cannot love the child and/or care for him, so they give him
up for adoption. And it is not for us to judge that decision. But
in many more cases parents can love and do try to care for their
disabled child, even when caring for him may mean custodial
placement.

In my earlier book, *Go Out in Joy!*, I wrote about the reactions of two mothers of disabled children. One little boy—who
is now in his teens—was born with spina bifida (myelomeningocele). The other little boy developed a severe seizure disorder
soon after birth, and subsequently died. (Not all children with
seizure disorders die as a result of them.) I'll quote from their
stories here, because of the light they may shed on the feelings
of your friend who has discovered her child is disabled.

Who expects that! I mean, you plan and pick out clothes
and blankets and set up a nursery and all that stuff. Your first
kid; you don't expect no trouble. You expect a baby, to bring
him home.
Oh, I'm not saying I never had fears. That's normal as you
go along. But myelomeningocele! I'd never heard of it, so
how could I worry about it. You know what I mean?

But they sedated me real good. I didn't know from nothing for days. I almost lost my mind when they told me. Started screaming and yelling.

I saw Joey. Lots of mothers don't. But he was bad. A lot of m-m kids don't look that bad. But Joey did. He got this hydrocephalus before he was born even. They didn't know if he'd live.

Anyway, they were afraid of me. I just started to scream. So they kept giving me stuff and giving me stuff to keep me quiet. I was real out of it.

And when I did come around I didn't want to see nobody, even Joe [her husband]. I mean nobody could do nothing. Nobody could change nothing. I'd have talked with anybody if it would have helped Joey. But I didn't want a lot of people shaking their heads and muttering how sorry they were. It wouldn't do him no good.

That's how I think I scared the priest out of his collar. God, when I think of it! I really didn't mean to, but I just didn't want to talk to nobody.

He knocked on the door . . . all in black with his black Bible and his stiff white collar. And he asked me if there was anything he could do. Like he was scared.

I told him, yeah, there was something he could do. He could get out and leave me alone and never come back.

And boy did he! He ran like a rabbit. He never came back, neither.

I didn't mean to do that. If he'd have come back I'd have apologized. But I was really out of it. And, well, he couldn't have done anything.

Each day Mark had a test. Then one day his mother said the results of one test had been sent somewhere in the West. Doctors there would look at them and maybe they'd be able to try some very new medication on Mark that might help. It would take a few days to find out.

I was sitting in the small waiting room talking with several mothers and fathers when Dr. Jenssen and Mark Heller's mother walked by. They went down the hall toward the other wing, then stopped and sat on a window ledge and talked. They talked for quite some time.

I watched out of the corner of my eye. Mark's mother

looked sad. Dr. Jenssen put her hand on the girl's shoulder, shook her head, and left. Mark's mother sat a few minutes on the window ledge, then walked back to her room. She looked at me for a moment when she walked by, but she didn't stop. She left the door to her room open. I wasn't sure whether or not to go in. But I did. The open door . . .

"Are you okay?"

She shook her head no.

"Would you rather be alone?"

No again. "Could you please close the door." Choked.

I did.

She was like a little girl, like me the night Ethel Stone died, needing to cry but needing someone to cry on.

I sat down on the daybed beside her and she simply buried her head in my arms and wept . . . and tried to talk at the same time.

"They can't do it . . . it won't help . . . no use . . . they said there's no use . . . won't help. I wanted it to work . . . to try . . . just try . . . it was the last hope . . . last hope. Now there's nothing. They've tried everything . . . nothing more . . . they can't do anything more . . .

"How can I tell Barry . . . my husband . . . how can I tell him?"

She sat back, blew her nose, wiped her eyes. The worst was over. And just beginning.

"Is that what Dr. Jenssen was telling you now?"

"Yes. She tried to be nice. But she said the doctors in the West said the new medication won't help Mark . . . He's incurable."

It took everything inside her to form the word *incurable*.

"All we can do now is take him home."

I looked at Mark. He was asleep in his crib, eyes closed, hair tousled, light perspiration on his forehead, little blue sleepers with firemen on them. No wonder it hurt. He *looked* so normal, so healthy, so cute when he was asleep.

"He wasn't like this from the beginning. He was so normal . . . for a whole year. Nothing wrong . . ."

Then the entire story—the story which she had been afraid that verbalizing would somehow negate the last hope—came out, now when there was no "last hope" to tease the superstition.

"One day he had a seizure—just like that, out of the blue. It scared me, but the doctor said just to watch him. Then he had another one six weeks later, and another one two weeks later. That one lasted six hours. Six hours. I felt so helpless. My own little baby. And I couldn't do anything. Nothing.

"He hasn't stopped seizing, really, since. He's on lots of medication now, but even that may lose effect sooner or later.

"I don't think he even knows us any more. I hold him and talk to him and kiss him and love him . . . And he doesn't even know I'm his mommy. He'll never know. Never."

She got up and put her forehead down hard on the railing of the crib . . . as if she wanted to bang her head against something in utter desolation. I watched as one of her tears fell from her cheek onto the crib railing and trickled slowly down the metal bar.

I heard how Mark Heller's mother felt. I saw how Mark Heller's mother felt. Never, never could I, in those moments, *know* how Mark Heller's mother felt.

But seeing and hearing were enough.

"How do you think your husband will take it?"

"He'll try to be brave because of me. He always is. I love him for that. But I know how it hurts him inside.

"But there's something more. Something I'm even more afraid to tell him." She measured out the words as if talking in rhythm with a metronome. "Dr. Jenssen said since she and the other doctors can't determine what caused Mark's seizures, they can't be sure the cause isn't genetic. Which means we can't be sure if we had another baby it wouldn't develop the same thing. So she suggested we not have any more babies maybe . . .

"And Barry and I wanted five children." The tears came again. "We both wanted five children. We decided that the day we got engaged. We've built our lives around that. Even moved to a suburb we didn't especially want to live in just because we could afford a down payment on a bigger house . . . with more bedrooms . . .

"And Barry's father. He can't even admit there's anything wrong with Mark. He talks to him and plays with him and brings him toys . . . even though he never responds. He says it's a 'phase' he's going through. He's sixty-two years old. He has to know better. But he won't admit it. He's his first grand-child.

"And the neighbors. They look at Mark funny when I take him out. I hate that. I guess you can't blame them. We haven't lived there long. They don't know. But they're so obvious. All I want to do is take him for a walk, for some air. Just leave us alone.

"Now it won't change. Sooner or later I'll have to tell them. They'll build it up, too. I hate that. If they just wouldn't look, would just leave us alone. 'Can't he walk yet?' 'Can't he talk yet?' 'How old *is* he?' 'Well, some children are just slower than others. He'll come along soon.'

"Just leave us alone!

"My mother said we'd have to put him in a home if they couldn't give him the medication. I can't think about that yet. Just an hour ago I still had hope. I can't put him away, not in an hour. I want him at home. I don't care. Barry understands. He says I don't have to put him anywhere I don't want to. Do you think I should put him in a home?"

Pause. "I think that's something you may consider at some future time. But I don't think now is the time."

"But do you think he'll have to be placed someday?"

"I'm not a doctor, so I don't know. But I can see you love Mark very much, which means you want the best for him, that you want him to be as happy and comfortable as possible under the circumstances. As long as that is with you and your husband in your home, then that's the place he should be. But if the time should come that you couldn't care for him prop-erly, for one reason or another, you might want to consider placing him. But I don't think you have to rush into anything. Look at some homes after a while. Talk with staff. See the children. See if they look happy and cared for and loved. Take your time."

"If I were *sure* he didn't know us, absolutely sure, it wouldn't be quite as hard . . . someday. But I wouldn't want him to think we'd abandoned him."

"Yes, I can understand that. But sometimes children are happy, too, with other children in a place equipped to their needs. I'll tell you a story one of the parents here told me one time.

"He had a cousin who was retarded. The parents of the

cousin had kept the boy home until he was sixteen, and they just couldn't handle him any more. Finally they placed him— with great fear. All the while they worried they hadn't done the right thing.

"But then the child came home for Christmas vacation. One day the parents saw him sitting unhappily by the Christmas tree. They asked him what was wrong. 'Mommy, Daddy, I love you but when can I go home? I want to see Billy and Freddie . . .'

"The boy was so happy where he had been placed that he called it 'home.' And rather than being hurt, the parents were happy because it made them sure they had done the right thing for the boy they loved.

"It's hard to know what's best all the time. But you love Mark. You'll know if the time comes to place him. I'm not worried about that."

"I guess so. I just have to keep telling myself this is it. We go home. This is it. I guess I still really don't believe it. I guess I still expect Dr. Jenssen to come through the door and say, 'I made a mistake. We *can* treat Mark.' But I guess, too, I know she won't. I think I knew that all along. I guess I want to pray now."

We did.

Mark Heller went home the next day.[6]

The emotions of these mothers are part of their mourning process. Each woman was coming to terms with the fact that her child was disabled, and what that would mean in lost and changed hopes. Mrs. Collins was describing her shock at discovering Joey's disability at birth. Mrs. Heller was at that point where her hope changed from hope for a cure to hope that Mark could go home and live out his time in peace.

To be a friend to someone mourning a disability in her child, listen without offering pity or clichés of hope; listen without offering advice on care; listen without judgment; and listen for optimism and hope.

Mourning disability in a child can be overpowering at first, but can often recede more quickly than expected because the child himself is there, and in need of being loved.

Your friend needs freedom to mourn, to vent anger, guilt (usually not based in fact), fear, self-pity, hopelessness, and the wealth of other normal mourning reactions described earlier. But she also needs room to practice loving her child and redefining her hopes for him and their life together as a family. So listen for where she is each time you talk with her. One day she may be mourning more than hoping. But the next day the balance may have changed, and she may be more optimistic. It is her journey; and it is a long one, filled with many peaks and valleys. Let her lead the way.

If you can be a "doing" friend for your friend with a disabled child, it is usually a great help.

You can help your friend with housework, grocery shopping, or other chores, freeing her to spend more time with her child and with other family members.

But there will also be times when your friend needs to spend time *without* her disabled child or other family members. Or times when she and her husband need to be away from any and all children. Getting a sitter for a disabled child is not always easy. If you can do so now and again, offer to sit with your friend's disabled child.

Many people want to help this way but are afraid they'll further hurt the child; or they think that care of a disabled child can only be done by a skilled professional. (If that's the case, there are a lot of parents and siblings of disabled children out there who should be granted professional degrees!) This is rarely the case.

If your friend feels comfortable teaching you the basics of her child's care, and if you are willing to learn, *you can be of more help than you know* by staying with him now and again while your friend enjoys some R&R. Do this for only a short time at first, say a half hour to an hour, until you all feel comfortable. As you would if caring for any other child, be sure emergency numbers are by all telephones and that you know the routes to all exits in the house.

The better you get to know your friend's disabled child, the more you will value him for, rather than in spite of, who he is. Soon you, too, will feel genuine hope for him in his life—measured with a differently calibrated yardstick, perhaps, but hope nonetheless.

Any human being's accomplishments should be measured in terms of his abilities. And those accomplishments should be equated in value not with the amount of money or power accumulated, but with the ability to affect persons and situations in this world with love or for good. If we can remember these things in measuring the accomplishments of disabled children—and of each other—we may see a lot more hope and fulfillment in the world.

On the other hand, to offer clichés of hope for your friend's disabled child is unfair. To say, for example, "Why, he'll be dressing himself in no time," when Johnny may have pulled up a zipper one inch after days or even months of practice, isn't fair to Johnny's accomplishment. Rather, one must realize the tremendous ability, strength, and concentration that that one inch took, and congratulate Johnny for this—his true accomplishment using all his current abilities. "Johnny, that was great! That took a lot of strength and patience. You're terrific!"

There may be places or doctors not yet tried that could help your friend's child. But unless you are *certain* your friend wants to hear about these from you or wants you to help investigate them, move *very* cautiously about offering care advice. I can think of friends whose advice I'd welcome with open arms if I discovered I had a disabled child. But I have other friends, whom I value very much, who nonetheless just wouldn't be the ones whose help I'd want in that particular area.

If you do feel you have information or know-how to investigate such matters, wait for a comfortable moment—usually not immediately after the disability is discovered, but maybe weeks or months down the road—to introduce the subject. Do this when you're *sure* your friend is able to hear and focus on what you're saying. Then you could say something like, "You know, Alice, I enjoy researching things. You may already be doing this or have asked someone else to do it; but if you ever want me to check out what other parts of the country—or the world—are doing to help children in Johnny's situation, I'll be glad to."

Alice may welcome your offer. She may not. If she doesn't, just let it drop and change the subject.

Regardless of her decision, don't be judgmental. She's doing the best she can, and that's likely a lot more than you or anyone else outside the family will ever know.

Grandparents of children with disabilities deserve a special word here. It's their lineage that grandchildren keep alive. They too invest great amounts of hope in the future of the newborn.

They, too, will mourn in a very real and valid sense when it is discovered their grandchild has a disability.

If your friend tells you that her long-awaited grandchild has a disability, realize you can help her a great deal by asking about the child not only that one time, but often thereafter, and by taking time to listen to what she has to say.

Sometimes grandparents are included in the gathering of family support that emerges when a crisis hits their adult children's families; but sometimes they're not. Distance may be a factor, or time. Regardless, your friend with a disabled grandchild will need an outlet *in her own circle of friends* to talk out her mourning—and eventually her renewed hope. Soon, with luck, she'll be bending your ear off in typical grandparenting pride! There is a newsletter, "Especially Grandparents," which is ". . . for and about grandparents of children with special needs." For more information write: Especially Grandparents, 2230 8th Avenue, Seattle, WA 98121.

Onset of a disability is reason to mourn. But as with any disability that does not result in death, it is a long road from that onset—often at birth—through the day-to-day living of life.

Mourning usually will end in redefined hope and healing, even if the disability does not go away. But mourning will make many return visits during the life of the disabled person and her family.

To be a friend to your friend mourning her child's disability, listen as much as you can. Try to pick up on any optimism and hope she may be feeling, without offering empty clichés of hope. Listen without being judgmental, without offering pity, and without offering constant advice on care.

And when you can, help her out by doing—especially if that doing can involve care of her disabled child from time to time.

My mother used to say to me, "I wouldn't give two cents for another child like you. But I wouldn't take a million dollars for you either."

Your friend with a disabled child would likely say the same thing.

BROKEN LOVE

A great deal has been written about divorce and other broken love relationships, and there is no intent or desire to repeat or digest that material in this section. As a minister I have worked with people going through these painful experiences; but divorce counseling itself is not my area of avocation or clinical expertise.

However, divorce is one of the major non-death causes of mourning today. And it can be problematic, because with divorce or other broken love, as with non-death disability, there is no traditional, socially accepted or defined route for mourning.

A *good* love relationship becomes as much a part of us as breathing itself. It feels natural and uncomplicated and free—a rhythmic part of our very being, giving meaning and wholeness, energy and calm, and above all, giving the sense of safety and invulnerability that comes with belonging.

Sensing a closeness with God can give this same feeling and more. But few people fully translate that into their lives or find it a satisfactory daily compensation for a love we can touch.

The problem, of course, in wanting a love we can touch is that in such a relationship all the players are human. And as a lot, we humans are not as good at sustaining love as God is. Consequently, more often than not, we end up in "less-than-ideal" love relationships, which ultimately break up, or else go on in "quiet desperation."

And when this happens, knowing God is still there and loves us (for those who believe so) still doesn't really help enough in the short run to negate our need to mourn.

> Missing your love
> with God's so
> close at hand.
>
> It seems somehow
> a sacrilege . . .
>
> but I think
> He understands.[7]

As cited earlier, one problem with trying to mourn the end of a painful marriage or other broken love is that there is nobody to bury, no wake to attend, no grim reaper to blame, no disabled limb to focus on. So, hope of reconciliation can persist a long time. "Could the clock be turned back? Could things get back to normal?" And until that period of ambivalence and ambiguity ends, mourning cannot really begin, and hence healing will be delayed.

Your friend very likely will want to talk, seemingly incessantly, about the lost love. Part of what she may be doing is letting the fact of loss sink in. How can you help a friend mourning the end of a particular love relationship?

A. *Listen*
    1. . . . to your friend
    2. . . . to his or her spouse (who may also be your friend)
They may need to ventilate:
    a. Anger
    b. Guilt
    c. Loneliness
    d. Hurt
    e. Feelings of worthlessness and/or failure
    f. Complaints of added daily burdens
    g. Fantasies and fears
    h. Sexual needs
    i. Illness, fatigue and/or sleep problems
    j. Inadequacies
    k. Martyrdom
    l. Real or imagined emotional cruelties
    m. Battles over money and/or children
    n. Repetition of the above
    o. Repetition of the repetition
    p. Repetition of the repeated repetition
    q. Et cetera
B. *Don't talk*
    1. . . . against either party or take sides.
    2. . . . about either party to the other, or convey information between them.
    3. . . . or act unkindly to either party.
    4. . . . with other people about the breakup or divorce. (In other words, don't gossip.)

C. *Do Talk*

1. . . . nonjudgmentally with the same sympathy and honesty you would use in other mourning.

2. . . . in situations where fear, guilt, anger, doubts about the meaning of life, and other powerful emotions are expressed.

3. . . . about the need for caution if your friend is seriously considering a major change (remarriage, move, job change, etc.) before the relationship has been over one year.

4. . . . about yourself and your life as things begin to return to a sense of normality and your friend begins to heal.

Shock, hurt, and healing are all part of mourning broken love, as are feelings of anger, rage, guilt, hopelessness, lack of self-worth, failure, blame, fear, fatigue, anxiety, and restlessness.

The denial and numbness of shock can last a long time if there is a prolonged period of uncertainty about the eventual fate of the relationship. In many instances those involved in a deteriorating relationship tend for a while to deny any problems to both themselves and to others—sometimes until long after such problems are visible to people outside the relationship.

But unless asked for advice on whether or not you feel professional counseling could help (it usually is worth a try), don't otherwise intrude in any seemingly deteriorating situation. You may find that one of the parties will turn to you for advice; or will ask you to agree that something her partner did was terrible; or will question you about her partner. *Don't get involved.*

Tell your friend that this situation is too important for you to risk influencing her thinking in any way. Suggest instead that she see a therapist or clergyperson. Tell her you're always willing to listen, but that as a friend you care too much about her and her partner to risk doing or saying anything harmful to their relationship. *And stick with it.* Don't weaken. Listen, but don't talk.

An irreversibly deteriorating love is an extremely volatile situation. Trying to find someone or something to blame is a big part of the mourning process. If you, as an outsider, choose to open your mouth with advice, gossip, or judgment, you know what could end up in it.

At some point the breakup of the relationship will become

public knowledge. The couple ceases to live together, divorce papers are filed, children may be resettled.

For some people mourning broken love this is the *trigger point for belief* that the relationship is truly, irretrievably over. For others, hope of mending is still too great. "It's only a nightmare. One day I'll wake up and it will be over."

Even if your friend *tells* you the relationship is over, that does not necessarily mean she believes it. (And it may not be.) At this juncture there may be a great pressure for you to take sides or convey information. Don't.

Of course, there are certain circumstances involving abuse when taking sides (providing shelter, medical help, etc.) or conveying information is necessary. But if it is a situation of gossip or angry/hurt feelings, don't take sides. Don't talk. Listen.

A person mourning a broken love in many cases *talks incessantly* at times, especially during prolonged shock/denial and again in parts of the hurt phase of mourning. This incessant talking can become boring despite your eagerness to help by listening. You may begin to try to avoid your friend or go to extreme lengths to keep the topic of her situation or her lost love from cropping up in your conversation.

But this is exactly when your friend truly needs you the most. She is so *very, very* lonely, and so vulnerable. She needs to feel she belongs somewhere. And in talking to someone else at least we belong to a conversation—even if it is one-sided.

Your friend may even try to transfer to your relationship with her certain experiences she shared with the lost partner: cocktails every evening at six; grocery shopping every Saturday morning. It won't be the same for her, of course. But that won't keep her from trying, because the need for normal patterning in her days is so great.

By doing that she may also be attempting, though not consciously, to make the event itself the key thing rather than the person with whom she is sharing it. This won't work either, because cocktails or shopping were fun because they were done together by two people who loved each other, not because they were cocktails or shopping.

That doesn't mean you shouldn't join her in some happily remembered activity. Just be aware that you are probably a necessary but inadequate stand-in.

There is one danger to this attempt to transfer pleasant experiences to someone else: it can lead to rebound relationships. You may not be available for a "love" relationship to replace the one that was lost. But someone is. And your friend may be so lonely, so needy and longing, that she may be vulnerable to love on the rebound.

If you see this happening to your friend, you *owe it to her* to suggest she see a counselor—if she isn't already doing so—before she formalizes the relationship. This is about the only "interfering" action that I would suggest you initiate during the entire process.

How you offer this suggestion is very important. Don't "put down" the new relationship or the new person, and don't tell your friend she "shouldn't" be involved in the relationship. These are judgment calls which are not your business to make. It may not necessarily be the new person who is the problem—it could be the timing.

Pick a calm, quiet environment when you both have some time. Tell your friend you're pleased that she is making new friends and that she seems especially happy with Bob. Tell her you are concerned *only* about the possibility that she may be rushing things. This is because you have read that most professional counselors recommend that a person make no major changes in his or her life for the first year after such a stressful event as death or divorce or broken love. Tell her you care about her as a friend. Suggest she talk with a therapist or clergyperson for a current professional perspective on mourning loss and suggested times for healing and making life changes.

Finally, tell your friend this is the *only* time you'll mention the subject, and that you'll be her friend regardless of whether or not she acts on what you suggest.

Above all, stick to this promise. Don't mention the subject again unless she does, and then follow her lead completely—don't offer anything more than you're asked at any time.

I am certain I'm on shaky ground with some professionals in suggesting you intervene in this area—or similar areas of precipitous action, such as selling a house, changing jobs, or making any major life change before the end of the first year after a broken or lost love. But having done so professionally a number of times, I have without exception, so far, had mourners thank me later for suggesting caution.

It is not *abnormal* to want to get rid of a hurt by quickly filling a void with love for someone new, or by placing ourselves in a new environment that offers us opportunities to feel in control, in charge of our lives again. But such precipitous new relationships or changes will not erase the pain or negate the need to mourn the loss; and they could possibly lead to additional pain or unhappiness. In most cases, if the new relationship or change was "meant to be" it will still be possible after our loss passes the one-year mark.

All in all, with this one exception, I suggest listening and not talking as the key in trying to be a friend to your friend mourning a broken love. At times "doing with" can also help as long as you aren't trapped into an expectation of routine performance with which you may not be willing or able to comply.

When your friend begins to talk more frequently and regularly about things other than her lost love, you have a good sign that healing is on the way. If she is able to remember and focus more on the good things that came out of the broken relationship, that too is a good sign. And if there was a situation that called for forgiveness on her part and she is beginning to be able to offer it, she is *well* on the road to healing. Giving forgiveness is one of the biggest vacuum cleaners for bad feelings known to humankind. But it is easier, unfortunately, to talk about than to do.

With many people mourning a broken love there won't have been the long period of isolation and withdrawal that usually accompanies mourning a death. So it won't have been difficult for you to have kept the doors of communication open.

However, it is just when you think things may get back to a semblance of "normal" between you and your friend that your whole relationship could change, and even die.

Your friend may need to do two things to help herself regain balance and move toward a "new" life. She may have to develop a new group of friends, usually divorced like herself or single; and she may need *not* to see some of the "old" friends she was especially close to during her divorce or breakup because of the pain she associates with seeing them. Both of these situations are normal.

Though difficult, the best thing you can do now is give your friend room and freedom to change, while continuing to make it clear that you would like to see her when she has time. Send a note. Grab a quick lunch together and let your friend guide the conversation, which will probably be about new people in her life and new "groups" she's involved with. Try not to take it personally if she makes you feel left out or unappreciated. Smile and show happiness for her in her newfound pleasures.

If you are married, invite her to a dinner party, either alone or with a guest of her own choosing. Don't matchmake for a long time unless asked. (Some counselors would say don't matchmake ever. But I met my husband in a "match," and he's not too bad! So I won't say "never.") If your friend accepts your invitation and comes alone, good for her! So what if you have an extra place at the table? Is that a reason to exclude a friend?

In time, your friend will heal. She will acquire some new friends in the process and give up, by choice or circumstance, some "old" friends. But if you've stood by her without judgment, without gossip, without denigration, without constant advice, and with a lot of listening, your friendship has a good chance of emerging intact.

Your friend may discover being unmarried or unattached has its merits. She won't be the first person to do so! If she is happier in her new single situation, respect this. There are few things more boring than a married or attached person who assumes every unattached person around him needs a mate for true happiness.

The important thing for you and your friend is *your* friendship. That's where to focus your energy. The love of true friendship can be a long-lasting gift if nurtured and respected. In fact, often the love of true friendship lasts longer than the "great loves" of our lives.

CAREER SETBACKS

Everybody dies or knows somebody who has. Almost everybody knows somebody who is divorced, or soon will be. But *not* everybody knows someone who was fired or "forcibly" retired from his job, especially after a number of years of service.

Being fired after reasonable length of employment is like having to sit in the middle of town with a sign over your head reading "Inadequate." No matter how many friends bring you sandwiches and coffee, and no matter what a great person they tell you you are, you still have to sit there in the middle of the town with that "Inadequate" sign over your head. And if you have to sit there long enough there is a real danger people will take your position for granted and forget that you haven't been sitting there for most of your adult life.

It is this doubt about his worth, brought home and made public by his firing, that may shadowbox with your friend long after he loses his job. And if a person feels he has lost his self-worth, he has a right to mourn.

To be fired from one's job does not of course mean one is unworthy or inadequate, either as a human being or as a worker. But if a person's *primary source of identity* is as Jennifer Smith, Vice President; or Harvey Bellows, Foreman; or Frank Cain, Farm Owner . . . if his self-esteem is closely linked to his job; and if he loses that job—he will have lost a large measure of self-worth. He will label himself as inadequate—someone "fired" or "let go." And the label will stick until he is given permission and support to mourn his loss, even if he gets another position in the interim.

To be a friend to someone mourning the loss of a job, *you should give him permission to mourn.* This is the main point of this section. And giving your friend permission to mourn the loss of his job will mean a lot of listening. Today. Tomorrow. And for many more tomorrows. Follow in general the advice on mourning in earlier chapters. And bolster your friend's self-esteem whenever possible *without patronizing or pitying him.*

Sometimes giving a person "permission to mourn" loss of a job takes a special skill. Mourning can seem weak to your friend at a time when he needs to feel strong. Often a person doesn't want to admit he's feeling inadequate and frightened. Many times, too, a person will feel compelled to display strength for the sake of family and community image.

This is not all to the bad. Keeping a positive outlook can actually help. But a positive outlook and a display of strength still won't negate the *valid* need for mourning the identity and self-esteem that were lost along with the job.

Help your friend know that it is not weakness to mourn the loss of something of value. And give him opportunities to mourn—*always* in a safe environment.

Also, let him know it's not weak to seek counseling for himself and his family to get through the rough time.

Like people mourning other major losses, your friend and his family will need to talk out angers, fears, guilts, inadequacies, etc. But your friend may not have many friends who will perceive this need and give him room, freedom, and permission to do so. Or, your friend and his family may not feel able to talk openly about such a "humiliating" subject. Professional counseling with a therapist or clergyperson may then be necessary.

If your friend is in financial difficulty and you can help or arrange help *and are comfortable and realistic about doing so*, then do it. Loaning money to a friend is not always wise. But it is not always unwise, either. You will have to be the judge.

Once I needed money and a friend loaned me some. "Don't repay *me*," he said. "But someday before you die I guarantee you you'll meet somebody else who needs some money! Repay me by giving to him; and tell him to repay you the same say I'm telling you to repay me."

My friend was right. I did meet someone who needed some money a few years later when I was in better financial shape, and I did "repay" his loan to that person with the prescribed message. This is a wonderful way to receive and give help, when it is possible.

If your friend loses transportation and needs help getting to job interviews, give him a lift if you can.

If your friend gets another job reasonably swiftly, that will help. But don't assume it will end his mourning overnight. He will probably still need to mourn his old job, his anger at being fired, and his loss of the old daily routine and faces.

Congratulate your friend on his new job; but give him freedom to continue to talk about and mourn the loss of the old one.

If your friend doesn't get a new job quickly, or at all, hang in there with him without patronizing or pitying him. If he seems to be stuck at a particular spot of mourning—like the pain of anger—keep listening to him without pushing him on. But strongly urge him to talk with a professional counselor.

Here you could say something like, "George, I can see you're still really angry about this. You're a reasonable man, so I'm sure there's cause for your anger. But it seems to be eating at you so, and not really helping. Why don't you talk it out with somebody who knows about these things. Pastor Roache seems to have his head on. Have you thought about talking it over with him?"

Don't suggest this more than one or two times. If your friend doesn't take your advice, at least you tried. Stick with him anyway as a friend.

If your friend can't afford to do all the things you used to do together, don't offer to pay each time in order to do the same things. Find different things to do.

An occasional treat is nice of course. But your friend will be feeling too inadequate to have to watch while you pay for bowling or golf or dinner each time you go out. (If you *can* pay for everything, you aren't a bad guy for wanting to do so. But know that few people will have their life values and self-worth so in tow that their pride can stand up to being on the receiving end all the time.)

Obviously, if you're in a position to directly or indirectly help your friend find a new job, do so if possible. But few people are in that position. However, more often than we may realize we do hear of job openings. It can just be a matter of keeping one's ears open.

To lose a beloved job is a valid reason to mourn. I tell my husband if he lost his job he'd be more broken up than if he lost me. And though he denies it and though I know he loves me, I haven't a doubt that what I say is true. His primary identity comes from his job. And there are thousands upon thousands of men and women out there just like him.

If you have a friend who loses his job, help him mourn the loss. Don't patronize him or pity him or embarrass his pride too often by playing Daddy Warbucks. Urge him to seek professional counseling if he has trouble mourning. And help him know that it is never weak to mourn the loss of something of value.

We love those people and those things in our lives which contribute to our identity and self-worth. And when we lose them, we mourn. To mourn the loss of a beloved job is okay, normal, and necessary.

8

The Sympathy Note

REGARDLESS OF WHETHER they have an ongoing close relationship with someone in mourning, most people would like to send thoughtful notes at the time of death to express their sympathy. But wrestling with what to say can be painful, and many well-intentioned people simply end up writing, "our deepest sympathy to you and your family," or they buy a special card that says that for them. There is nothing wrong with either of these. It is still a way saying you care.

But if you want to write a note or add a note to a card, here are some suggestions.

Don't think your adjectives are too gushy. There is a limit, of course; but the person in mourning will feel devastated. His loss will be so great to him, and the person who died so perfect for a time, that what may sound flowery to you very likely won't to him. The first time he reads the note it may not register at all. But the second time he reads the note he may be in the pain or ache of mourning, and its sentiments will be in tandem with the very deep and strong emotions and memories he is feeling.

Write what you feel. If you feel the loss was huge and that it must be a terrible experience for the person in mourning, say so. Your not saying so won't make is less horrible, and your saying so will confirm the validity of the person's feelings.

Write the words "died" or "dead" rather than "passed on" or "was lost." "I'm so sorry to hear that John died." The person may have passed on, but he had to become dead here on earth to do so. He may be lost to us, but he's lost because he died. ''Dead'' is indeed a stark word, but using a softer word won't change the reality or lessen the pain, it will only feed the denial.

Don't be afraid to mention the dead person's name in your sympathy note. To those mourning him he will always have a name, and it will give them pleasure to see it in writing.

One of the most poignant things I ever heard was a comment by a parent mourning the death of her child. ''You know,'' she told me, ''one of the little things that bothers me most . . . I never see my son's name written any more. It's not on report cards, or Christmas card addresses, or in the Little League standings. Sometimes,'' she admitted sadly, ''I just sit down and write it myself, just to see it.'' This is something you may wish to keep in mind when addressing the newly widowed. To you ''Mrs. John Smith'' may seem to be a diminution of your friend's separate identity. But even women who generally preferred being known as ''Mary Smith'' may wish to see their husband's name on envelopes addressed to them in their time of mourning.

If you remember something particularly nice about the person who died, especially in relation to the mourner and especially something the mourner (if it is an adult) may not have known about, tell her. (If the note can become a sympathy *letter*, all the better. The person will have a lot of time to read and reread it.) For example, suppose you and John were shopping on the way to lunch one day and he became so involved in getting Mary just the right birthday present that he made both of you miss lunch. Does that seem trivial? It won't to Mary. Tell her about it. Couple it with how much John loved her and how everyone knew what a good thing she was in John's life, ''the best thing that ever happened to him!''

You have now given Mary a story she will enjoy hearing about John; reinforcement from someone else who knew how much John loved her; and confirmation that she has been a good wife—all in strong, superlative adjectives. Also, Mary has had a chance to see John's name written in conjunction with hers a number of times in the letter. And she has seen it written that he is dead.

Some traps people fall into in trying to write sympathy notes—or in talking—are: Trying to lessen the mourner's loss by outdoing or equaling it; implying that the dead person can be replaced; implying that the loss was less because the duration of the relationship was short; or telling the mourner he will "grow" or "learn" or be a "better person" as a result of enduring the loss.

People trying to diminish the loss by outdoing it may dwell on how much they loved the dead person, how close they were to him, and how hard his loss is for *them*. It may be a great loss—and in occasional cases it may even be a greater loss than that of the primary mourner to whom the sympathy note is written. But it is useless to say so or imply so. One-upmanship can only do harm here, even when it is offered with only good intentions. If you are writing to a person in mourning, write to that person about that person, not about yourself.

Telling about a similar loss you may have experienced at another time won't help ease the pain either. That was your time and this is the mourner's time. She won't be helped at this juncture by hearing the details of your experience. Sometime later this may help; but not right now, not right after the death.

It is *never* wise to imply that the dead person can be replaced. Those we love are not replaceable. One of the most common but perhaps worst situations in which to suggest this is when parents have lost a child. So many people mean well and write or say something like, "But you're young, you can have other children," or "At least you have other children at home," as if the child's death can somehow be less awful because there are or can be other children. Suffice it to say that parents of a child who dies don't see it that way.

A similar situation can occur with parents of a child who dies at birth or shortly thereafter, or one who is lost through miscarriage. Many well-meaning people say, "Well, at least you didn't really get to know your baby (or know him very long) so you don't have all that love and all those memories." Love for a child is an absolute. It's not based on cause and effect. And remember, too, that the younger the child who dies, the closer he is in a physical sense to his parents. He gets one hundred percent of his needs met by the parents. The mother in particular may still feel the child as an extension of her own body. It is only as the child gets older that he begins to separate from his parents, and they to see him as his own person, apart from them.

Death of a child or any other person who is loved is never easier for the mourner because of age, or number of siblings, or any other rational factors. To try to soften the pain of death by introducing any of those well-intentioned rationalizations not only won't work, but will make the mourner feel alone and misunderstood in his pain. Don't try it.

The mourner may indeed "grow" or "learn" or be a "better person" as a result of enduring the loss. But it is far too soon—the time of writing a sympathy note or talking with someone in the shock or hurt of mourning—to say so. In fact, it is usually best to wait for the mourner to say these things first. If he does come to be able to see something good which emerged from his suffering, that is a sign of healing. You can then support and reinforce his positive feelings without denying the depth of the suffering.

A footnote about sympathy notes and children in mourning: It can be a nice thing to send a second sympathy note directly to the child if you know her. This, however, should be very simple; something like, "Dear Mary—I know you loved your daddy very much. I'm so sorry he died." If the family is religious you could add, "I will think about you and your mommy and your daddy in my prayers." Close with "fondly" or "with love"—if the relationship is close enough.

If you are very close to the child, you can go into more detail. But regardless, avoid in any way trying to compete with the child's own memories of the person who has died. And, in this instance, avoid phrases like, "I know your daddy loved you very much." This can, of course, be true, but children are sometimes reluctant to think that their parents said something about loving them to someone they don't know that well.

Children can be loathe to share any part of their parents with someone else. It's hard enough to share them with brothers and sisters, let alone adults they barely know (or even those they know well).

Writing a sympathy note or letter or adding one to a commercial card is not easy. But it can mean a great deal to a person as he reads and rereads his sympathy mail during the mourning process.

Commercial sympathy cards used to be terrible, and there are still some of those around. But there are also some truly lovely and beautifully written ones. And if you decide you just cannot write a note, at least write in longhand somewhere on the printed card, ''I send my deepest sympathy to you.'' That much personalization anyone can do. But give a note a try—you may surprise yourself.

9

Ongoing Thoughts About God and Suffering

I believe that somewhere there exists an answer, but that the wrong questions are being asked; or even that no question is needed.[8]

Either a person believes in God or he doesn't. No one can scientifically prove or disprove the existence of God. When I first went to work as a student chaplain in a hospital unit where children were dying from brain tumors and suffering severe permanently crippling birth defects, the "problem of pain," as C. S. Lewis calls it, hit my belief in God smack in the face.

If God is all powerful and all loving, which I believe Him to be, if God is all powerful and all loving—why? Why does a nine-year-old child suffer two years of pain from a brain tumor and then die an agonizing death? Why is a baby born with an open, oozing spine that could leave him paralyzed and a swollen head that may render him retarded? If God is all loving and all powerful, why?

I was still asking that question several years later in an advanced training program at the same hospital. And nights like the one I describe below brought me little closer to any answer. (Names and other identifying details have been changed.)

The father had a miserable time finding a parking place. The huge University Children's Hospital had no parking lot then.

162

Finally he found a vacant, metered parking spot eight blocks away, threw in four quarters for two hours and headed into a January wind toward the hospital. He figured two hours would be long enough. They would probably examine his baby, give her some medication for the flu—he hoped not a shot—and send them home. Eight blocks back to the car for him, he thought.

In the emergency room his wife was talking to a doctor with a heavy black moustache and black, wavy hair. She looked worried. But he figured she would be reassured by the doctors at such a good hospital. And perhaps here they could find a local pediatrician for Rebecca now that they were moved and settled. No use running back and forth to Wisconsin any more.

One hour later on the parking meter Joe and Carolyn Wyler were told that Rebecca, their only child, had less than twelve hours to live. The "flu," with sudden onset, no warning, had really been acute myoletic leukemia. It was raging through the baby's body. There was nothing the doctors could do but give her oxygen to make her more comfortable. There was nothing the parents could have done to prevent it.

I was the chaplain on call, and I was called. And I watched for the next ten hours as those parents in complete shock used the core of their faith to exist.

Would I baptize Rebecca? "We don't believe she'll go to hell if she's not—we couldn't believe that with her—but we would like to give her to God since we know she's going to go to Him so soon."

Tears came; and the parents, probably twenty-one years old at most, held on to each other.

Rebecca had huge brown eyes and soft brown hair; a tiny bundle lying still in the junior crib that usually held older children with leukemia. She breathed into a green, plastic oxygen mask. That was the only sound in the room. Her father and mother held hands and each took one of Rebecca's tiny hands. "I baptize you in the name of the Father, and of the Son, and of the Holy Spirit, Amen. May the Lord Bless you and love you, and keep you in His heart forever, Amen."

As I kissed the baby's pale little check, I felt as though we were all in a film, and soon the lights would go on and a voice would say "cut." But no lights came on and no voice was heard. Rebecca's mother and father kissed her and held on to each other and cried. I left them to themselves, as a family, and I cried in the stairwell.

Why, God, if You are all powerful and all loving, why? You couldn't want an eleven-month-old child so much that You would cause that much pain to her parents. You couldn't be punishing her for some major sin. An eleven-month-old couldn't have committed one. You couldn't be using her to punish her parents for something, for that would be denying her an existence in her own right. It couldn't be because of lack of faith, because her parents are "churchgoing." And besides, where would that put Your Grace?

Is it that You are not all powerful or that You are not all loving? And if You are both, then how could this be? And, once again, why?

Besides spending what time I could with Rebecca Wyler's parents that day, I was being paged frequently to the Intensive Care Unit (I.C.U.) to sit with the nearly crazed mother of a five-year-old girl who was in her last days of dying. The child had had a number of heart surgeries and her mother was almost uncontrollable, continuously pacing outside the I.C.U. between the then-allowed visiting times of fifteen minutes every other hour.

The mother went the gamut, from bargaining with God to venting her anger at God, to giving herself to God—all the while making me promise that they had kittens in heaven, because she felt guilty that she hadn't bought her daughter a kitten. Since I was the chaplain, she said, I could promise her that there were kittens in heaven and she could then tell her daughter, who was in a coma.

"The other chaplain didn't know whether there were kittens in heaven or not. He's supposed to know. How could innocent little kittens not go to heaven, just like innocent little girls like Sally? Tell me there are kittens in heaven."

If God is all powerful and all loving, why?

As this conversation occurred outside the Intensive Care Unit at about nine-thirty that evening, a doctor motioned for me to come into the unit.

"She's dying," screamed Sally's mother, "she's dying and they won't tell me."

"Sally's not dying, Mrs. Hansel," the surgeon said to the

mother; and to me, as the plate-glass and wood door closed behind us, "at least not tonight. But someone else is."

"Rebecca Wyler? Now?" I asked, a knot forming in my stomach.

He looked puzzled. "No, I don't know her. I mean Joshua Brown; he's over there." The surgeon pointed to a crib where a tiny baby lay naked. A few electrodes were placed on his chest and a respirator tube was in his mouth. "He's on a respirator. His EEG (electroencephalogram) has been flat for three days—absence of brain activity equaling brain death," he kindly added the explanation I already knew. "I just thought you should know. His parents are very religious, they're on their way now and we thought you should be here."

I guess I looked pale or shaken or stunned, or all of the above. "The other baby you mentioned," asked the doctor, "is she dying now too?"

"Yes, tonight sometime, probably soon."

"That's too bad," he said, "if you can't handle both we won't ask you."

"No, that's okay, I'll do my best. I'm just kind of surprised, I guess. I hadn't known about Joshua."

"Sorry we didn't tell you sooner," said a nurse who had joined us, "but we figured Mrs. Hansel needed you more. Or, *we* needed you to be with her more."

"Thanks," I said, and we all smiled weakly. That was to be the only smile of the night for any of us.

"We've slowly been preparing Joshua's parents," the doctor continued as we walked to Joshua's bed. "They've been with him a lot and seen him like this for the last three days, with the flat EEG and all. They know. When they left yesterday they said to call them when he dies."

I was just about to ask how one could tell when a person on a respirator that did his breathing for him had died—when the doctor began removing the monitor wires, pulled away the green plastic tube and said, "Well, that's it." The baby gasped a few times, like tiny convulsions, and then lay still.

I couldn't move. I hadn't expected it. I didn't know the baby, I didn't know his parents, and I had just watched him die. I had just watched him being unhooked from the respirator. I had just watched the plug being pulled.

In the state of Illinois it's legal under certain circumstances to pull the plug when the brain is dead. No crime had been committed. I knew that, but I hadn't been prepared.

Yet, reflecting on this days later, I realized that the doctor and nurse had told me what was going to happen, they just hadn't said it in so many words. And, without saying so, they had wanted me—as chaplain—present. I guess it was hard enough to pull the plug outright, without having to say it outright, too. But after being with Rebecca Wyler's parents and Mrs. Hansel all day I had little ability to read between the lines.

Somebody tapped me on the shoulder as I stood dazed beside Joshua Brown's bed while the nurse bathed him. "Excuse me, but you have a phone call."

"I do?"

"Yes, it's four-west." Four-west, where Rebecca Wyler was. She couldn't have died, not yet, not in the same moment Joshua Brown died. No.

"This is Nina. . . ."

"This is four-west." The voice was serious. "Rebecca Wyler just died. Her parents would like you to come down and pray for her with them while she's still in her room. Can you come right away?"

"Another baby just died here, too." I guess I said it to myself, to the wind, as much as I said it to the nurse on the phone. "I think I can come now, but let me check."

The nurse who had called me to the phone had heard the conversation. "Go ahead to four-west, we have to finish bathing Joshua and get him ready for his parents to see. They aren't here yet. Just come back as soon as you can."

"All right," I said numbly.

When I reached Rebecca Wyler's room most of the lights were off. Little Rebecca lay covered by a soft yellow blanket, as if to keep her warm in the chilly room. Her eyes were shut and the green plastic oxygen mask lay to the side of her face, useless. The room was still except for muffled sobs from Rebecca's mother and three other relatives who had come late that afternoon from Wisconsin. The sides of the crib were down; she wouldn't roll out.

Something made me take the parents' hands and kneel. They and the three relatives followed, our hands joined around the crib. The child was slightly above us. A street lamp shone through the window, making everything blue-white.

I prayed, as asked, for Rebecca's soul. And I prayed for her family, and thanked God for eleven months of joy. Eleven months. *Months*.

Why, God, why? If God is all powerful and all loving, why?

As I finished the prayer I saw that about ten of Rebecca's doctors and nurses had come in quietly. Some were crying, as were Rebecca's parents and her relatives. The doctor with the thick black moustache and wavy hair cried—the same doctor who had spent the last day of Rebecca's life with her; had spent her dying with her, though he could do nothing to prevent it.

Then Rebecca's mother sobbed a rattling sob and her husband circled his arms around her and they left.

"Thank you," Rebecca's father said to me. "Thank you for baptizing her and being with us and coming back now to pray again. We know that Rebecca is with God now, and we feel we sent her back to Him right."

I bit my lip until it bled to keep from crying, and ran back up to the fifth floor Intensive Care. Why, God? Why?

"Doctor Martin is with Mr. and Mrs. Brown now, bringing them back to see Joshua," said the nurse. "I'm so glad you're back."

As she said that a large woman and her short, slender, balding husband came through the door of the unit with the surgeon. He obviously had told them that their son was dead.

Dr. Martin introduced the parents to me and as we walked toward the baby's bed the mother said, "My Joshua, he's with Jesus now, he's with Jesus."

Then she gently reached down and picked up her little naked, dead son and held him in her arms and sang "Sweet Little Jesus Boy" to him more beautifully than I've ever heard it sung.

By this time I wanted to cry so much that I ached. I wanted to run and cry—or scream. I just bit my lip more.

Joshua's mother finished her song and kept rocking the baby in her arms, and we prayed for him.

Finally, his father took Joshua gently and kissed him and laid him back in the crib. "Come on, Mama, your other children needs you; I needs you."

But as they neared the door of I.C.U. Joshua's mother turned to me. "You know the Twenty-third Psalm, don't you, child? Will you say the Twenty-third Psalm for me? Will you say it for me right now?"

I started to say the Twenty-third Psalm. And the large, sad woman buried her head on my shoulder, atop my intensive care gown, and sobbed and held on and sobbed. I finished the psalm while stroking her head. Same question, God.

They left, Mr. and Mrs. Brown, to go home to their other children. When I turned to look back, Joshua Brown was gone from his crib.

I was about to go and just sit down somewhere, but I didn't get the chance. A loud buzzer suddenly went off and the doctors and nurses raced to Sally Hansel's bed like bullets. She had had a cardiac arrest. But I couldn't even react. I just stood there and watched.

They got out those paddles, put them on her chest, and gave her a shock. They did it three times before she started breathing again.

I found I couldn't assimilate the possibility that Sally Hansel might die that night. I couldn't imagine being present for a third death in an hour.

After the final paddle shock the staff began to repack the equipment and move away from Sally's bed. Her cardiac machine was beeping regularly again; the little girl with the blonde curls and her brother's pictures pasted on her crib was still breathing.

Suddenly a buzzer went off again, but this buzzer was behind me. The staff, with the equipment only half packed, was already touching the paddles to the chest of a child I hadn't even noticed before. She also had blonde, curly hair, and appeared to be about six years old.

"God, not Melanie," someone said. This time it took two shocks and Melanie was breathing again.

Melanie was Melanie Herd—someone told me when the crisis was over. She was six years old and had had major cardiac surgery that morning. All had been going well, everyone thought, but now something had gone drastically wrong—like a major heart attack; and they were afraid she was dying.

In fact, Melanie Herd was dying, probably within a half hour to forty-five minutes. Could I please stay? They weren't expecting this . . . the parents weren't expecting . . .

I just nodded. I.C.U.—two. Four west—one. A resident was sent to find the Herds and bring them back to Intensive Care. Dr. Miller wanted to talk with them away from the other parents in the waiting room, talk to them and try to prepare them. A necessary, but impossible task.

How did Dr. Miller feel that night? In less than one hour he had had to pull the plug and let one child finish dying, then only minutes later see another child, for whom he had had hope of life, die too. All as he stood helpless despite his training and skill.

Was God all powerful and all loving in Dr. Miller's mind that evening?

A buzzer went off again. It was becoming old hat. Little children stopping breathing, dying, all in a night's work. This new child was in the crib where Joshua Brown had been less than a half hour earlier. The child had come from another hospital, probably to die at Children's, someone said. I hadn't even seen him come in. This time it only took one shock with the paddles. "Looks like he'll be okay tonight," said a resident I hadn't seen. "Thank God." Then he added, "Melanie Herd's dying."

I nodded. "Dr. Miller is with her parents now, I think."

"Good."

Just then Melanie's parents walked in from the anteroom with Dr. Miller. They looked ashen and angry and scared, like wild animals suddenly put into a small cage. They walked with Dr. Miller over to Melanie's bed, kissed her, and she died, just like that. Dr. Miller took them back to the anteroom and told them they could see Melanie once more if they wanted to after the nurse had disconnected all the monitors. They said they wanted to. Then he asked me if I would stay with them while they waited. Of course I would.

All of us were in shock—Melanie's mother and father, and, by now, me. If we had been in touch with the violence of our feelings, we would have been screaming and kicking out at things. But we sat there talking, calmly. That's shock.

Mr. and Mrs. Herd sat there and told me Melanie's whole life story, all six years of it; just talked and talked. They told me about their farm downstate, and about how this operation was their last hope. They said how they could hardly believe it when the doctors told them the operation looked successful; and how by evening they had just been allowing themselves to begin to believe it. And now . . .

I sat there and listened.

Then the nurse came and Melanie's parents went back in and kissed her good-bye.

I asked them if they wanted to pray. They didn't want to pray.

"There can't be a God," said Melanie's father. "But if there is and He let this happen to Melanie I couldn't believe in Him anyway. No; thank you for being with us, but we don't want to pray. We just want to get out of here and out of this city, and never come back."

Melanie Herd's parents left, just as Joshua Brown's parents and Rebecca Wyler's parents, with their children dead in bed behind them. God—three, parents—zero. Or was it God—two; parents—zero? Do only believers' children go to heaven?

Or is it God—zero; parents—zero?

For centuries, religious scholars have been trying to explain how suffering can exist in a world created by a loving and all-powerful God. It would be easier not to ask the question at all. It would be easier to say that God works in mysterious ways. And many people are more comfortable doing that. And that is all right. It is frightening to ask "Why?" It is frightening to ask "If God is all powerful and all loving, why?" Especially when there is no provable answer to the question.

It is frightening to ask such a question because if we look at our world as it is—three innocent children dying within an hour like so many ants, nuclear threat, drugs, murder, rape—you know the list. . . . If we look at our world as it is and try to understand why, we might come to the conclusion that God doesn't exist at all, or if He does, He cannot be both all powerful and all-loving. For assuming God does exist, it would seem that if He were both all-powerful and all-loving, the magnitude of his love would *force* Him to use the magnitude of His power to keep at least so-called "believers" from suffering.

But believers do suffer and innocent babies get sick and die or starve to death, or get killed. So, many people find it safer or more comfortable not to ask the question in the first place; to have faith and hold on to the mystery instead.

It has been a good number of years since that night at University Children's Hospital when Rebecca Wyler, Joshua Brown, and Melanie Herd died within one hour, and in the interim I have known scores of children and adults who have suffered and died or who are yet suffering. In those years I have not lost faith, but I have not stopped asking why either. Nor do I apologize for the question or for still getting angry with God at times in the face of unexplainable suffering.

But when all is said and done, I still believe God exists. And I still believe God is *total power and total love*, not limited power and selective love.

Along the way somewhere, however, it occurred to me that something was wrong with my question: "If God is all powerful and all loving, why?" Not that something was wrong with me for asking it; but that something was wrong with the question itself.

One day I wrote out the question, then I eliminated four words, one suffix, and one question mark and found something that made more sense to me.

If God is all powerful ańd ǎll lovińg, ẃhý?

God is all powerful love.

In other words, all God's power is all God's love, and all God's love is all God's power. *God's power and God's love mean the same thing.*

And that began to eliminate my question in its previous form. I believe God is all powerful and all loving. But His power *is* His love, and His love *is* His power.

God's power cannot, therefore, cause human suffering because that power is love, and love cannot cause or allow suffering. That is something we are eager to believe, for no one wants to believe that God would cause him to suffer to punish him for sins, or teach him a lesson, or test his faith.

But God's power also, therefore, cannot perform miracles of a nature that cannot be performed by love. And this is more painful for us to believe. For we would all like to think that it is possible for God to do anything in this earth, whether it's moving mountains or curing illness.

To bring this thought down to earth, let me use a simple illustration: A mother who loves her child would not cause that child to be hit by a car—not even to teach him a lesson about the dangers of crossing the street or to test whether he had learned his lessons on crossing the street.

But unless that mother eliminates all cars and other dangers and controls the movements of her child for every day of his life, she cannot guarantee that her child will be safe.

And if that mother could eliminate all dangers and could

control the movements of her child each day of his life, that would not be loving him. It would deny the child—the human being—the chance to become a person in his own right, and would instead turn him into a puppet controlled by a benevolent puppeteer.

God obviously has not eliminated all dangers from this world. Nor has He created us as His puppets. We are free in each moment, in each decision, to respond to the power of God's love within us and to let it grow, or to deny it.

But regardless of our choices, we cannot destroy it.

For those who believe in God, this whole earth, a place inhabited by man and beast and nature, evolved from the atom of God's love. It has taken on its own identity—land and sea and creature, and our fathers and our fathers' fathers. And though the world changes every day, and though many of its inhabitants stretch and groan to achieve power apart from love, that atom of God's love remains.

This world still has not been able to overcome the power of love; nor to control, create or manufacture its essence. Love alone still roams free through the earth and in the hearts of mankind. Moving in its quiet way, given far less recognition than its daily displays deserve, *love is the only living thing in this world that has lasted since the beginning of time. And will last.*

Though the power of love does not move earthly mountains, the power of love is immeasurable. If the child mentioned earlier is injured by the car but not killed, he will draw strength not only from the healing powers of medical science, but also from the power of his parents' love.

How much greater still is the strength that can be drawn from the power of God's love? For even if we have *no one else* from whom to draw love for strength and healing and renewal, we can draw all of these and more without measure from God. And in doing so we can know that we are not and never will be alone; that we are not and never will be without the essence of love.

God's love cannot cause the sufferings of this earth, nor can it eliminate them. But God's love can give each of us the miracle of overcoming suffering, if we let it.

And I saw the seeds of such a miracle that night years ago at Children's Hospital in Mr. and Mrs. Wyler and Mr. and Mrs. Brown. The miracle of that evening was that two families, in complete emotional shock, when they could not act with their own power, chose to act in the power of God's love.

"Why?" is a question each parent very likely asked many times later. And I'm sure anger came also. And neither the Wylers nor the Browns were able to alter the fact that their children were dead, just as Melanie Herd was dead.

But though it was a fact of earth and not the power of God that took their children's lives, it was the power of God and not a fact of earth that acted within the Wylers and the Browns that night. This power of God, called upon in free choice by each parent, gave them the conviction that death is not the end, and the faith to release their children to God.

We are all residents of a strange world that contains much suffering and pain, disfigurement, mental anguish, violence, and early death. But people such as the Wylers and the Browns, by calling upon the power of God's love within them, *have overcome the ultimate evil of this world while still living in it*. And that is something that cannot be explained. It is a miracle.

For the love that is God's power is not only something that comes when we die; it is the love, and power—the source for miracles—that we have *now*.

This was described to Christians by Jesus Christ and sent to us in fire. But sadly, many of us treat it as the poor and unheralded member of the Trinity. The love that is God's power is the power of the Holy Spirit, the power of the Comforter. The miracles that can occur on earth today are miracles of the Spirit— miracles of our spirits wrought of the love of God made manifest in the Holy Spirit.

The power of God's love is just as strong now as it was nearly two thousand years ago when New Testament writers illustrated it in the miracle stories—stories of Jesus performing miracles of the flesh. God made flesh manifesting His power in the flesh.

But the purpose of the miracle stories was to teach us lessons about the power of God's love. Jesus told the people this over and over again.

And He told us that the *ever-present continuation* of God's love for us would be the Holy Spirit, the Comforter. In future the miracles of the power of God's love—if "miracles" we need to call them—would be miracles of the Spirit.

But we Christians still brush most of that message aside in a crisis and dwell on "miracle" almost exclusively as something to be made manifest in the flesh. We await the moving of mountains, the cure of illness, the elimination of suffering and death. And when it doesn't happen, we ask, "Why?"

I still ask, "Why?" And I still get angry and take that anger out on God. And I still know that if I were paralyzed or dying, or my loved ones were, I would hope for a miracle of the flesh as well as a miracle of the Spirit.

But at times now I am able to stop asking, "If God is all powerful and all loving . . . before I ask my 'why?' " At times now I am able to feel that all of God's power is all of God's love, and that the potential of that atom of power, that atom of love, in our lives and in this world is greater than any miracle of the flesh—if only we would use it on ourselves and each other.

Can any of these thoughts help someone who is dying or in mourning?

If people feel, as Melanie Herd's father did in his anguish, that there is no God, telling them that there is a God and His love can be a healing power is rarely something to do in a moment of crisis. They may be polite; but they will not believe you and they will not want to hear you. You may even cause them additional pain if they fear that it is because they are not believers that their tragedy had befallen them.

What you can do is *stick by* the person in mourning or who is dying *regardless of the differences in your beliefs*. Don't sell short the value of your own beliefs. But don't be judgmental or holier-than-thou with your friend. Just stick by him. Perhaps the day will come, if he is open, when you can slowly begin to plant seeds of belief here and there, if by no other means than your gentle, ongoing support.

How can you help someone in mourning who *does* believe, but who is angry with God or who, in guilt, fears he is being punished by God?

If one uses the premise that all of God's power is all of God's love, then divine punishment for sins real or imagined is not the cause of anyone's physical suffering. A person does not suffer and die from cancer because God is "getting him." Most people will tell you they know logically that God does not cause suffering to punish us for our sins. But regardless of their logical knowledge a great number of people, deep inside, still wonder what they "did to deserve" their suffering; what they did so awful that God caused or allowed them to suffer this much. This is a normal reaction.

In the Christian faith the dilemma of suffering was addressed in the life and death of Jesus Christ. Jesus was sinless, yet He suffered and died.

Not only did Jesus not cause suffering; He removed it. As the spirit of God made flesh, He performed miracles of the flesh. But still He suffered and died.

The New Testament writers tell us that as He performed these miracles Jesus often said, "Thy sins be forgiven thee." But this was not to say that a sin committed by the person had caused that person's affliction. Rather, it can be argued, it was to say that each affliction was a *sin in itself*, a "sin" that by the nature of this earth had happened to the human being.

And God, manifested in the flesh in Jesus Christ, manifested the power of His love in the flesh. To God in Jesus Christ there was no difference between saying "Thy sins be forgiven thee" and in saying, "Rise, take up thy bed and walk." The sin—the affliction that had caused suffering—had been cast out.

This world and we humans bring enough suffering, enough sins, on ourselves that God doesn't have to cause or allow more to be added to them.

So if you discuss the issue of punishment with your friend in mourning or your friend who is dying, this may help you reason her out of believing that God is punishing her. The final belief decision is hers; but offering options of thought can be helpful if she is not forced or rushed.

If one believes all of God's power is all of God's love then one cannot believe that God causes or allows any human suffering, whether for punishment, or to test our faith, or to teach us a lesson, or because He had limited His power.

The power of God's love is total. It is boundless and unconditional and everlasting. There is no amount of sin in any of us or on earth that can be large enough to override the power of God's love or cause it to bring us harm.

That is not to say that God approves of the sins, the sufferings we cause ourselves. Love cannot approve of harm or condone wrong. But God will cling to the frail, damaged, thwarted vestige of His atom of love in each of us, and hope that we will someday give that love room to grow within us and beyond.

Even if your friend is able to believe in the power of God's love to overcome the evil of her tragedy, *it will not negate her need to go through the mourning process,* although it may indeed shorten the process. For in fact, the reason your friend is mourning at all is precisely because love does exist. One does not mourn the loss of something or someone one does not love.

Furthermore, if your friend does display strong faith it can be dangerous to keep congratulating her for it. If you keep saying, "I admire you for your faith," this gives Mary little opportunity to turn to you later if and when she does get angry with God or begins to question her faith. And that can happen to even the strongest of believers. If it could happen to Jesus, it could happen to any of us.

Tragedy is a time of testing. It's not God who tests us, but we who do the testing. We test who we are, what we believe, where we can find hope, faith, and love. If you hang too heavy a halo on your mourning friend, she may feel she cannot risk this testing if it involves any questioning of God. This can hinder her mourning, and could damage your friendship.

You don't need to shield God from your friend's questions. God's love can be tested a million-million ways; it will never be found lacking. *What is lacking is our use of the power of God's love in our own lives.*

Be patient with your friend in mourning or your friend who is dying. Give her room to breathe and a listening ear that does not judge. If she needs to verbalize any questions she feels about God and faith and religion, let her. Jesus questioned. Why should we expect more of our friends than God asked of His Son?

10

A Death

Many professionals believe that children with terminal illnesses know they are going to die, either at a conscious or subconscious level. This may well be true, but I'll walk alongside the bandwagon for a while longer unless "subconscious" is defined very broadly.

Be that as it may, I want to tell you about one little girl I knew who was quite aware that she was dying, and about how she prepared to meet God.

Death did not come peacefully for Taffy. Taffy was eight when she died. She lives in the recesses of my heart in a wild and free way, racing through when I least expect her, giving meaning to the term "bittersweet" memory. I have never been as close to any other child who died. Taffy knew she was dying, she wanted to talk about it, and like the Lone Ranger, she chose me as her Tonto. We went through together to the end . . . almost to the end.

Taffy's parents were divorced. She never mentioned her father; he never visited, and I never asked. Her mother came often in the beginning of Taffy's illness. But each hospitalization following the end of each remission brought fewer and fewer visits from Taffy's mother. Taffy's mother and Taffy loved each other dearly. But her mother could not talk with Taffy about what was happening to her, despite attempts by Taffy and even gentle hints by hospital staff.

Most of this occurred before I met Taffy, and I was only told of it. I saw her mother only once, the week before Taffy died, visiting Taffy with three other people. But I'm getting ahead of my story.

I met Taffy when I was beginning my advanced pastoral education year at University Adult and Children's Hospital, having finished the stint of basic hospital chaplaincy training. I'm not sure which unit I was assigned to when I met Taffy, but it was not the leukemia unit. Taffy had leukemia, but I didn't know that when I met her. All I knew that, like a great number of other children at Children's, she had very little hair and she raced about the hallways in umbilical-like tandem with her intravenous pole, bottle, and tubing.

Taffy almost always had some fluid dripping into her arm. And rather than forcing her to stay in bed all the time the nurses hung the bottle from an IV pole on wheels and let her roam her unit pushing the pole and its apparatus along with her. Taffy's IV pole was so much a part of her that one could almost cease to see it.

I first remember Taffy from a Sunday morning chapel service I conducted in Children's Hospital. She was eight years old and had been in the hospital this admission for three weeks.

Had she been in before?

"Oh, yes, lots of times," she said.

She had come to the service by herself, no adult or nurse accompanying her. She sat very straight in her chapel chair, IV pole before her, and watched me with huge brown eyes. She never smiled.

As we went around in a circle so each child could talk to God, Taffy prayed, "Dear God, please let heaven be happy." It was a prayer I didn't forget that morning. But I didn't pursue it, or Taffy.

If she had been on my unit, I rationalized at the time, I would have found her later that day and talked with her about heaven, about her strange little prayer. But I had that excuse—she wasn't on my unit—and I took it. I put Taffy and her prayer somewhere off to the side. Besides, I probably wouldn't see her again anyway, I reasoned; I didn't have a chapel service assignment again for a month.

But that same week, as I was rounding a corner toward the elevator, I heard a small voice.

"Hi, will you come and see my pictures?"

I looked down and there she was, the little girl who prayed the haunting prayer about heaven.

"You were in chapel, weren't you?" she asked me.

"Yes," I said. That's my line, I thought to myself.

"I like you," she said straightforwardly. "Will you please come look at my pictures?"

"All right," I agreed, and let her lead me to the four-east playroom. "I remember your name, it's Nina. Do you remember mine?"

I didn't. There were umpteen children in chapel I rationalized to myself, how could I be expected to remember? But I wished I had.

"No, I'm sorry, I don't," I said, "but I bet it's a pretty name." I tried to soften the blow.

"It is a pretty name, I guess. It's Taffy. Will you remember?"

"Yes, Taffy, I'll remember. I promise I'll remember."

"Good." Suddenly she stopped walking and looked up at me. Her hair was soft brown and very short. She was more bone than skin. Her cheeks were hollow and pale. Her large almond-drop eyes were serious and questioning. She reminded me of a tiny waif in a hungry-children ad.

"Will you be my friend?" she asked quietly.

It surprised me and undid me a bit. I remember thinking, Taffy, you have leukemia and I'm not assigned to the leukemia unit and the head chaplain will have my head if I start to visit you. "Thou shalt not cross the boundaries of thine unit into another chaplain's unit except in emergencies," sayeth the chaplain director. And *no* room was left for the human variable. I would be taking my professional life at Children's in my hands to agree to be the friend of a child not on my assigned units.

But God, or at least something more sensible than the iron-clad rules of the chaplaincy department, told me that this was an "emergency," that it was all right to respond to her need.

So I bent down to waif height and looked at Taffy's serious face. "Thank you, Taffy, I'd like that. I'd like to be your friend."

And that's what happened, Taffy and I became friends. It was a very personal friendship. We didn't share it with the world. We kept it between us for special times and special circumstances; and in the long run it served us both well.

Taffy had had leukemia for nearly five years. She'd been in and out of Children's more times than anyone could remember without checking. As I mentioned, no father was in the picture, and her mother was at times too overwhelmed by it all to be very hospital-visible. So Taffy did it herself. When in the hospital she hung in there herself, she and her IV pole. It made her wiser than her eight years.

But deep down it also made her more needy than a toddler. And for some forever unknown reason, Taffy had chosen me to be her friend, her friend unto death. I didn't know that yet as she pushed the IV pole with one hand and dragged me by the other into the four-east playroom that late fall morning to see her pictures. I only knew that I sensed her request was important enough to break an intractable rule.

Her pictures were done in crayons and watercolors. They were extremely happy, with suns and flowers, birds and trees. Each one had one person in it, a little stick-figure girl with long black hair. "That's me," Taffy explained. "My hair was like that; I was real pretty. Mom said I would have been beautiful but I've got leukemia so I guess I won't be."

"Does that make you angry?"

"It did at first when my hair fell out, I was really upset. My hair was beautiful. Sometime when we're better friends I'll show you the picture of me with my hair. You won't even know it's me. Anyway, I guess I'm used to it, but I still cry about it at night sometimes. I liked being pretty. Don't tell anybody, please, I mean about my crying. It's better not to."

"Is it?"

"Most of the time. Most of the time it is. Will you come and talk to me when you can?" She changed the subject.

"When I can, Taffy." I went along with the change. "But let me explain something to you so you'll understand." We sat down in the playroom. "There are five or six students chaplains at Children's and we're each assigned to a different unit. I'm assigned to four-west and somebody else is assigned to four-east [her unit]. Now, that doesn't mean we can't be friends, but it does mean you'll have to understand that I may not be able to see you as much as we both would like."

"I know how that works," she nodded. "My chaplain has talked to me. She's a Sister. She's very nice, but she's too stiff. I tried her, but she doesn't hear what I'm saying. I tried you just now, you did. Please be my friend when you can."

How hospital-wise she was! "Okay, Taffy." I smiled.

I'm not sure how she had "tried" me but I think I can guess. If I had given an excuse for not remembering her name, or if I had said she was "really pretty now, too," when she was talking about her hair, she would have written me off. Any woman worth her salt knows when she's at her prettiest. And Taffy was indeed a woman worth her salt. I couldn't pull any punches with Taffy, and I never tried. That's a pretty good basis for all lasting friendships.

Whatever medicine was going from Taffy's IV bottle to Taffy that fall worked for a while. She went home about three weeks after we became friends. I never saw her mother in all that time. But Taffy didn't expect me to intervene with her mother. She understood and loved her mother, and tried to make things easier for her.

"My mother isn't very happy when I talk about dying. She tells me not to talk about that, not to think about it. I don't like to see her so sad, so I don't. But I do think about it. Can I talk about it to you when I want to?"

"Yes, Taffy, you can. Any time you want to. But Taffy, do you know why your mother has trouble talking with you about dying?"

"I guess because she loves me and it hurts to think about it."

"I think you're very wise, Taffy. I think probably that's the exact reason. But does that make you unhappy?"

"At times kind of. But I think I understand how she feels. I think if it were my mom dying maybe I'd be too sad to talk with her about it. So I guess I'll just have fun with my mom and talk with you about the other things. Will that make you sad, too?"

"Yes, probably at times. But no matter how much I may grow to love you it will never be like your mother loves you. That's a special kind of love and it can hurt most of all when we think of dying."

"I know; but I'm glad you're my friend."

"Me, too. Taffy, will you try to promise me one thing, though? You're going home soon. Maybe sometime your mother will feel better about talking with you about dying. If she seems to, will you give her some more chances?"

"Okay, but I don't think she will. I kind of tried a lot already. I think the doctors and nurses have, too, though they won't tell me. But it just makes her sad and she cries. So I stopped. I think they did, too. But she's really nice. Don't worry, Nina, I love her a lot. I'm not trying to get you to take her place. She's my mother, you're my friend. I won't forget. Okay?''

"Okay." No punches. She didn't miss anything. Eight years old, going on eighty.

And she didn't forget. And her mother never could talk with Taffy about dying. And though that was sad, it was probably the only way her mother could cope. And that left me with the gift of a special little friend who shared her ''insides'' with me.

"You're going to be here 'til June?'' Taffy asked me the night before she went home that November.

"Yes, until June twelfth.''

"Then you'll still be here when I come back.'' Statement. "Oh?''

"I heard Dr. Clayton say that was the last medicine. They've tried them all on me and when this one stops working they don't have any more. I guess I knew that all along this time. I figure it will work two or three months, four maybe if I'm lucky. So you'll still be here no matter what.''

"No matter what unless you happen to be wrong.'' I smiled.

"I won't be,'' she said almost matter-of-factly.

It was two months, only two months. January twenty-sixth she came back. We didn't see each other or talk to each other, or even exchange Christmas cards while she was at home. In fact, to this day I don't know Taffy's last name. I don't think she ever knew mine. We were hospital friends committed to living through, together, the dying of Taffy. And that's what we did, almost.

The oral page I received that January twenty-seventh was for an unfamiliar extension. It wasn't my new unit, four-center, or my old unit, or even my favorite unit, neurosurgery, that was calling. It wasn't the chaplains' office number. Probably a mistake, I figured, as I dialed 4971.

"Hi, this is Nina Herrmann; did someone page me?''

"Oh, yes, hold on a moment, please.''

"Hi, this is Lucinda Bowman. I'm a nurse on four-east. You're the chaplain who's Taffy's friend, aren't you?''

"Yes?'' I turned cold and waited.

"She came in last night. She wanted to find you. We walked over to four-west, but they said you had changed units. She'd like to see you when you have some time.''

"How is she?''

"Not too good. She can still walk, but I can tell it hurts her a lot. . . . You know there's nothing else now, no more medicine?"

"I know."

"I'm leaving here in two weeks and I'm glad. I don't want to be here. I can't stand it any more, especially a child like Taffy. I think I'll make it out before she goes, but not by much. Don't you ever wonder why? It's just not fair."

"No, it isn't. And yes, I do wonder why, all the time."

"Well, thanks for stopping by. I know she likes you a lot. That's everything now." She hung up. I was still cold.

Taffy looked terrible. I don't know much about leukemia, I never worked on that unit long enough to find out. I didn't know the treatments, I didn't know the symptoms, or the declining process, or what it looked like to die from leukemia.

And I chose not to ask. I chose not to read Taffy's chart or talk with her doctors and nurses about her daily condition. I just decided to be with Taffy and take things as they came. But in the two months she had been home her leukemia hadn't been kind to her. She looked tinier and more ravaged than ever as she lay sleeping in her white-sheeted bed. Her IV was permanently in her arm, so that they could administer all of her drugs without giving her separate shots all the time, which saved added pain. She had had enough pain already.

There were bits of blood in her nostrils. I assumed she'd had a recent nosebleed. I was right. But the nosebleed had been from coughing up blood.

"Hi, Taffy," I whispered. She opened her eyes.

"Nina, hi, I'm glad you came." She turned on her back painfully. "We tried to find you. I was afraid you'd moved. I was afraid you'd gone to another hospital."

"No, I'm just on four-center now. It's filled with little babies."

"I'll bet they're cute."

"They are, but they can't carry on a decent conversation."

She smiled. "Like I can?"

"Like you can. How are you?"

"Okay. My knees hurt a lot, but I can still walk. I really want to walk. I don't like staying in bed."

I remember how she was never in bed in the fall, always

running around the unit with her IV pole. "Do you want to walk with me now," I asked, "or shall we keep it 'til later?"

She hesitated a split second. "We can try it now."

"Taffy," I looked at her, "honest, remember?"

"Okay, maybe later then. I'm just a little sore."

I smiled outside. "Okay, later it is."

"Nina?"

"Yes?"

"I'm getting scared now."

"I know."

"Will you stay with me as much as you can?"

"As much as I can."

"What's He like?"

"Who?"

"God."

"Hmmm . . . I know what I think He's like. But why don't you tell me what you think He's like first?"

"Okay, but you'll tell me too, all right?"

"I'll tell you, too."

"I think God is big and strong," she said slowly, "and people want to touch Him and be where He is. I think He knows what I want—like my long hair back—and He'll understand and let me have it in heaven, at least I hope so. I think He won't let my knees hurt any more or let me be sick any more.

"I think He'll probably want me to do something for Him, too, but I don't know what.

"Oh, yes, and I think He laughs and will let me bounce on His knee. My friend's daddy always lets her do that and it looks like fun. What do you think God is like?"

"Taffy, I believe God is just like you think He is."

She looked at me, "Do you really?"

"Yes, but I will add one thing."

"Good, what?"

"Well, you said you think God will want you to do something for Him, too, but you didn't know what."

"Um-hum. Do you know what?"

"Well, I have a feeling I may. I think what God wants us to do for Him is love Him. First, to believe with all our might that He loves us no matter what. And then to love Him back in return."

She waited a long time. I could hear the lunch carts rattling up and down the hallway, but it was quiet in Taffy's room. Finally she said, "I love God; but do you think He really loves me now, the way I am now?"

"Yes, Taffy, God loves you now, just like you are now. And He always has loved you, and He always will. I don't know a whole lot else about God, but I know that without any doubt."

She smiled. She just smiled, the first real, true, open and complete smile I had seen from her that day. She closed her eyes and reached for my hand and fell asleep.

I sat there holding her hand in the quiet room. If I didn't believe God loved you, Taffy, I thought, I'd lose my mind. I don't know what causes leukemia or why little children or anyone suffers and dies, but I do know God doesn't cause it. I do know God loves us no matter what this free earth does to us or its free people do to each other. I know God's love is the one overwhelming reality that can bring peace out of chaos.

If I didn't know that, if I didn't believe that, I'd probably lose my mind sharing death with Taffy and the countless other dead children I have known.

Yes, Taffy, God loves you and He'll give you long hair and a ride on His knee, and peace, and a smile on your face.

It was easiest for me to spend longer periods of time with Taffy in the evenings, especially when I was on call. Then I had an official reason for being there. During the day I would see my patients at Children's and Adult hospitals, talk with some families in the early evening, then end up in Taffy's room after visiting hours when things were quiet on the unit, and when she'd be more frightened.

Her pain got worse every day. Soon she could no longer walk, or even sit up in a wheelchair. She was also on her last-ditch pain medication and it was a race to see if its effectiveness could hold out as long as her life. The sieges of blood-coughing were more frequent; and she was markedly weaker each day. But she didn't give up.

Taffy's greatest fear was of dying alone. She slept better during the day because people were around. Not visitor people, though; no visitor people for Taffy. Days went by without anyone coming to see her. But more staff, and other children's parents, and other children's visitors were around during the day.

Far fewer people were there during the night, so it was at night that Taffy was most frightened. It was at night time she was afraid she would be awake and alone and die. So we started a routine, Taffy and I. Anytime I could stay late, which was reasonably often, on call or not, I'd sit with her and rub her legs until she went to sleep. She'd really try to go to sleep, too. She didn't try to prolong my staying with her by staying awake. She simply wanted to go to sleep with someone sitting beside her holding her hand or rubbing her legs, or just being there.

For two or three days in a row in those long winter weeks, I'd be sure that death was near. Then she would feel better for a day or two. One of those feeling-better days she decided to give me a surprise.

I had told her I would stop by to see her after lunch, about one o'clock. Just before then, as I got off the elevator on my unit, here came Taffy around the corner to meet me, a nurse pushing her, sitting up in a wheelchair.

"You always come to see me," she smiled, "I thought this time I'd come to see you."

The pain of getting into that wheelchair must have been excruciating. She was propped up among what seemed like dozens of pillows. But she had done it. She had gotten up. This time she had come to see me.

"Taffy, you look beautiful," was all I said. And she did. And she knew it. She knew now what beauty truly was and she knew it was true.

Taffy's physical suffering only grew worse. I would make no additional point now by describing it. She still had relatively good days mixed in with the bad, but they were fewer. Still she hung on. And still we visited at bedtime. And still I rubbed her legs. We talked less and less. We had said most of what needed to be said. Sometimes she liked me to read to her, but mostly we sat quietly until she fell asleep.

One Friday in late February her pain increased noticeably. Her medication helped for shorter and shorter periods of time.

"It won't be long now, a week or two," a nurse told me as she saw me leave Taffy's room that Friday night. I knew she meant well, but I guess I'd rather not have known. Or I guess I'd rather not have had it confirmed.

Over that same weekend a strange thing happened. Visitors began to fill Taffy's usually empty room. She was in great pain much of the time but she tried to be polite. The visitors would try to tell her jokes and try to make her laugh. The voices in Taffy's room always seemed to be two or three levels higher than normal, and they were always upbeat.

Her mother began coming every other night from about 7:00 to 8:30. Other adult visitors would come and a number of Children's Hospital staff dropped by. My one-word association memory of Taffy's room that week is "crowded." I guess because before it always had been so empty.

There was a crowd with Taffy the last night I saw her. Her mother, some relatives, and friends of her mother and a hospital staff member had all stopped by. When I stuck my head in the door they were talking to each other and Taffy was propped up in bed trying to cough blood unobtrusively, as everyone politely glanced away at the ceiling or the floor and looked as though they wished she'd stop that.

"Excuse me," I said, "I didn't mean to interrupt." I smiled at Taffy.

"Nina, are you staying late tonight, will you come back?"

Since her mother and relatives were there I really hadn't planned to stay, but something in her voice made me decide to. "I'll be back later," I said, "I promise."

She smiled at me as best she could as I left. But sitting there propped up in bed she looked trapped and tired, overwhelmed and in pain—in very much pain. When I came back her pain was nearly unbearable.

"Hi, Taffy."

"I'm glad you stayed."

"So am I."

"What time is it?"

"About nine o'clock."

"Oh, a half hour yet." Tears just started running down her cheeks.

"A half hour until your medicine?"

She nodded.

"I'm sorry it hurts so much, Taffy, I wish I could help."

"Me, too."

"Do you want me to rub your legs?"

"I'm not sure. I'm not sure anything will help any more. Can you stay until I go to sleep?"

"Yes, I'll stay 'til you go to sleep." And with her pain I wondered if that wouldn't be all night.

"Oh, it hurts so much," she sobbed.

It must have because she couldn't keep from crying. She usually fought that back for all she was worth. And I couldn't even hold her in my arms because I knew that would just make it hurt more.

"What time is it now?"

"Two minutes after nine."

"Will you try rubbing my legs?"

"Okay."

"Harder, please."

I rubbed with literally all my strength.

"That's good, that helps." She grew quieter.

The shot came, then more pain, more waiting, more shot. It was near midnight.

"Will you talk to me? Will you tell me about God, about what you think when you think about God?"

"All right." I went on rubbing her legs. "Sometimes, Taffy, when I'm sad I just close my eyes and picture God the way I still like to picture Him best. I see Him with snow-white hair and a long white beard, wearing a very soft white robe. I can't picture His face much, only that His eyes are clear and kind. He's above me and I start to climb up toward Him.

"Sometimes I have to climb for a while and other times only for a bit. But each time, before I've reached Him, He reaches down and lifts me up, and I can feel cool air rushing all around me.

"And soon I'm nestled in the crook of God's arm, all snuggled in His soft white robe, and I take a deep, deep breath and feel very safe. And then I can rest.

"Sometimes He rubs my arm or my back or my head. Sometimes He just holds me tight. If I feel I want to cry, I know I can because He'll not push me away. He'll understand. Sometimes I tell Him how I feel—even though He knows—because I need to say it, to say how I feel. Other times I just hold on to Him.

"I see God like this when I'm happy sometimes too, Taffy. And then I sit up in His arms and tell Him and He smiles and laughs with me with His clear, happy eyes, and I feel even better.

"And you know, Taffy, sometimes even when I'm angry, when things happen I don't understand, things that don't seem fair, I crawl up and sit in God's arms and beat on His chest in fury. I know that doesn't change the things I'm angry about on this earth, but I still feel better just to have been free to get angry with God. I guess I know that even when I'm angry He'll still love me.

"Then after I've been with God a while, He lifts me up and holds me close to His chest, then slowly lifts me back down through the cool air to earth, and I go on. And I always, always feel better.

"But I guess the best times are when I'm sad and I feel alone and I go to visit God. It is then I know I'm not alone.

"I felt all alone tonight," said Taffy.

"Even with all your visitors?"

"I wish they had come last week or the week before. Tonight I only felt alone. Can I try to climb up to God?"

"Sure, just close your eyes and start climbing. He'll find you before you get very far."

The nurse came in at 12:30 A.M. with Taffy's medicine. Taffy was asleep. I left at 12:45. I never saw Taffy again.

In the movies she would have died peacefully in her sleep that night in God's arms. But she didn't.

The last evening I spent with Taffy was a Thursday. She died that Saturday night. I was away for the weekend. I had told her I had to be. But I didn't think she would die. It was the second time a child I had been very close to had died while I was away. But with Taffy the circumstances were different, and I found myself feeling far more guilty.

I didn't even find out Taffy had died until Monday. Another student chaplain told me that morning. He'd been on call and was there. He said Taffy went into a coma, but not before going through a delirium of pain. "It was awful," he said quietly, "just awful."

I didn't ask for details; I didn't want to know. I hurt too much and I felt too guilty. It was late that afternoon before I could even find a safe place to cry.

My being away had been unavoidable. I was giving a weekend seminar at a church convention, a long-term commitment and something I did all too rarely as it was.

But the religious excuse didn't help me. I was angry that I hadn't been there. I wanted to tell Taffy how much I loved her, how much she taught me and gave me. I wanted to kiss her good-bye. I wanted to see her alive just once more. And I couldn't.

But I felt most of all that I had let her down. I felt most of all guilty that I hadn't hung in there until the end, hadn't been her friend until the end, hadn't been with her at the most important time, at her death.

I was on call that Monday evening, sitting alone in the children's cafeteria thinking about Taffy. A nurse walked by, carrying her empty tray to a kitchen window. She stopped at my table.

"You know, don't you, that Taffy died Saturday?"

"Yes, I know, thank you," I said trying to be polite but really not wanting the intrusion. I recognized the nurse as the one who had brought Taffy's medicine that last Thursday. She turned to go on, maybe sensing I didn't feel like talking. But then she stopped and came back.

"Can I sit down for just a minute?"

"Sure." No, I don't want to hear the details, I was screaming inside. Go away, I feel badly enough as it is. Just leave me alone.

"I just wanted to tell you something," she said. "I know you weren't there when Taffy died and I have a feeling you wish you had been. But you were there when it counted. You were there all those weeks when nobody else was, when Taffy really needed somebody.

"She didn't need anybody Saturday night; nobody could do anything. Oh, there were tons of people there, everybody was there. Saturday and Friday, too; all last week. It always happens that way. They come out of the woodwork at the end, at the very end when they're really not needed.

"You were there when it counted. You were her friend and loved her. I know, we all did; Taffy, too." She picked up her empty tray and left.

How can you thank someone for something like that?

In my mourning I had found a friend, a stranger who knew what to say and when. And it made all the difference that Monday night and throughout my mourning of Taffy.

You, too, can say the right thing or do the right thing. You, too, can be a friend to someone in mourning. It can make a difference. It could make all the difference.

It is worth all the effort.

NOT THE END

NOTES

1. Granger Westberg, *Good Grief* (Philadelphia: Fortress Press, 1962), pp. 21-22.

2. Doug Manning, *Don't Take My Grief Away* (San Francisco: In-Sight Books, Inc., 1984), p. 99.

3. Anne M. Brooks, *The Grieving Time* (Garden City, New York: Dial Press, 1985), p. 28.

4. Ibid., p. 16.

5. Erna Furman, *A Child's Parent Dies: Studies in Childhood Bereavement* (New Haven & London: Yale University Press, 1974).

6. Nina Herrmann, *Go Out In Joy!* (Atlanta: John Knox Press, 1977), pp. 87-91, 96-97.

7. Melba Colgrove Ph.D., Harold H. Bloomfield, M.D., Peter McWilliams, *How To Survive the Loss of Love* (New York: Bantam Books, 1977), p. 78.

8. Christopher Leach, *Letter To A Younger Son* (New York, Signet, 1982), p. 134.

BIBLIOGRAPHY AND SUGGESTED RELATED READING

The Bible, Revised Standard Version. Nashville: Thomas Nelson Publishers, 1972.

Brooks, Anne M. *The Grieving Time: A Year's Account of Recovery from Loss.* Garden City, New York: The Dial Press, Doubleday & Co., Inc., 1985.

Cameron, Jean. *For All That Has Been.* New York: Macmillan Publishing Co., Inc., 1982.

Clardy, Andrea Fleck. *Dusty Was My Friend: Coming to Terms with Loss.* New York: Human Sciences Press, Inc., 1984.

Colgrove, Melba, Ph.D., Bloomfield, Harold H., M.D., and McWilliams, Peter. *How to Survive the Loss of Love.* New York: Bantam Books, 1977.

DeFord, Frank. *Alex, the Life of a Child.* New York: Viking Press, 1983.

Donnelly, Katherine Fair. *Recovering from the Loss of a Child.* New York: Macmillan Publishing Co., Inc., 1982.

Fanshawe, Elizabeth. *Rachel.* London, Sydney, Toronto: The Bodley Head, 1975.

Furman, Erna. *A Child's Parent Dies.* New Haven and London: Yale University Press, 1974.

Herrmann, Nina. *Go Out In Joy!* Atlanta: John Know Press, 1977.

Jones, Ron. *The Acorn People.* Nashville: Abingdon, 1978.

Krementz, Jill, *How It Feels when a Parent Dies.* New York: Alfred A. Knopf, 1982.

Kubler-Ross, Elisabeth. *Death, the Final Stage of Growth.* Englewood Cliffs, N.J.: Prentice-Hall, 1975.

————. *Living With Death and Dying.* New York: Macmillan Publishing Co., Inc., 1981.

————. *On Children and Death.* New York: Macmillan Publishing Co., Inc., 1983.

————. *On Death and Dying.* New York: Macmillan Publishing Co., Inc., 1969.

————. *Questions and Answers on Death and Dying.* New York: Macmillan Publishing Co., Inc., 1974.

————. *Remember the Secret.* Berkeley, California: Celestial Arts, 1982.

————. *To Live Until We Say Goodbye.* Englewood Cliffs, N.J.: Prentice-Hall, Inc., 1978.

Kushner, Harold. *When Bad Things Happen to Good People.* New York: Avon Books, 1983.

Leach, Christopher. *Letter to a Younger Son.* New York: Harcourt Brace Jovanovich, Inc., 1981.

LeShan, Eda. *Learning to Say Good-by: When a Parent Dies.* New York: Macmillan Publishing Co., Inc., 1976.

Lewis, C.S. *A Grief Observed.* New York: Seabury Press, 1963.

Manning, Doug. *Don't Take My Grief Away.* San Francisco: In-Sight Books, Inc., 1984.

————. *Comforting Those Who Grieve: A Guide for Helping Others.* San Francisco: Harper & Row, Publishers, 1985.

Marty, Martin E. *A Cry of Absence.* San Francisco: Harper & Row, Publishers, 1983.

Monjar, Stephen. "What Do You Say After You See They're Disabled?" Chicago: Written for the Rehabilitation Institute of Chicago, 1986. (Copies of this pamphlet may be obtained free of charge by sending a stamped, self-addressed, business-size envelope to: R.I.C. Division of Marketing and Communications, 345 E. Superior Street, Chicago, Il. 60611.)

Panzarella, Joseph J., M.D. with Kittler, Glenn D. *Spirit Makes a Man.* Garden City, New York: Doubleday & Co., Inc., 1978.

Pendleton, Edith, compiler. *Too Old to Cry, Too Young to Die.* Nashville: Thomas Nelson Publishers, 1980.

Sanford, Doris. *It Must Hurt a Lot.* Portland, Oregon: Multnomah Press, 1985.

Schiff, Harriet Sarnoff. *The Bereaved Parent.* New York: Crown Publishers, 1977.

Stearns, Ann Kaiser. *Living Through Personal Crisis.* New York: Ballantine Books, 1985.

Stein, Sara Bonnett. *About Handicaps: An Open Family Book for Parents and Children Together.* New York: Walker Publishing Co., Inc., 1974.

Weizman, Savine G., Ph.D. and Kamm, Phyllis. *About Mourning: Support and Guidance for the Bereaved.* New York: Human Sciences Press, Inc., 1985.

Westberg, Granger. *Good Grief.* Philadelphia: Fortress Press, 1962.

About the Author

Nina Donnelley received her master's degree from the Divinity School of the University of Chicago. She has been the director of the Department of Chaplaincy at the Rehabilitation Institute of Chicago for eleven years. Previously, she was a television news reporter in New York, Washington and Chicago. As a result of her training in hospital chaplaincy at the Children's Memorial Hospital, she wrote *Go Out In Joy!* Mrs. Donnelley lives in Chicago with her husband and two stepchildren.

Bring New Meaning
and Insight Into Your Life
with

BALLANTINE/

EPIPHANY BOOKS